How Do We Reach *Those* Kids

How Do We Reach *Those* Kids

Creating Places of Belonging
Where Everyone Learns and Thrives

Mary Duerksen Sklar

© 2015 Mary Duerksen Sklar

All rights reserved. Except as permitted under the US Copyright Act of 1976, no part of this publication may be reproduced, distributed, or transmitted in any form or by any means, or stored in a database or retrieval system, without the prior written permission of the author.

The names, events, places, and student writings have been fictionalized to protect the privacy of persons involved.

Printed in the United States of America
Printed on acid-free paper

Library of Congress Control Number: 2015907022
AR Publications, Pinole, California

ISBN-10: 0692440763

Cover designed by Adrian Graham Webster whose exceptional creativity, skill, and understanding contributed to the production of this book

To my beloved sons, Trey and Andy,
who first showed me how to teach
with relevance and relationship

And to my students who, in spite of incarceration,
trusted me with their stories
I hope this book will honor you.
Without you, I could not have learned
to teach this way.

Table of Contents

	Foreword	ix
1	Helping Kids Reclaim Their Lives	1
2	Lost in Society, Lost in School	7
3	Relevance Ignites Energy in the Classroom	13
4	Relationships	21
5	Respectful Interactions	27
6	Unique Classrooms	31
7	Classroom Seating	35
8	Roll Response	39
9	Quotes Painted on Walls	43
10	Poem Day	71
11	Change of Pace	75
12	Checking In	87
13	Hurt People Hurt People	89
14	Public Recognition of Success	93
15	Everyday Strategies	97
16	If We Always Teach Like We've Always Taught	101
17	Don't Teach a Class, Run a Program	105
18	The Worse It Gets, the Better It Becomes	107
19	*Those* Kids	109
	Epilogue	117
	Acknowledgements	121
	About the Author	125

Foreword

While I served as a juvenile magistrate, Mary Sklar's students were the young offenders who appeared before me daily in orange jumpsuits and chains. As a teacher for a juvenile detention center, Ms. Sklar was charged with the daunting task of providing educational services during incarceration to a youth population that included gang members, violent offenders, and drug dealers. The charges filed ranged from truancy to violent, criminal acts such as sexual assault, aggravated robbery, and attempted murder. It was not uncommon for her students to have been raised in abusive, neglectful, and broken homes or, alternatively, in the streets. Another teacher in the detention facility where Ms. Sklar works once told me that twelve years in that environment was the equivalent to twenty-four years of wear, tear, and stress on a teacher in a traditional classroom.

Although changing antisocial behavior was my primary focus as a juvenile magistrate, inspiring students to believe in themselves through the educational process was the sacred province of Ms. Sklar. Though our tools differed significantly, we did share a common goal: to disrupt the pipeline that sometimes leads a student from school to adult prisons. For when a student drops out, gets kicked out, or turns off from an educational system that brands them as one of *those* kids, he or she is easily drawn into and enamored of the universe of crime. Hope for many students sometimes turns into bitter despair and alienation.

Drawing on fourteen years of institutional experience, Mary Sklar has provided an invaluable instructional guide that not only underscores the importance of creativity, experimentation, and imagination in a classroom, regardless of its physical location, but her guide also provides concrete examples how new as well as veteran teachers can enhance a student's learning experience and also help a student to reconnect to the excitement, pleasure, and enjoyment of learning.

As you read her book, Ms. Sklar's genuine and authentic passion for her students and her love of teaching can readily be discerned. The tools she shares, if implemented, can enrich any student's life. More important, her guide will help teachers reach those kids who initially appear unreachable. Any teacher who stays in the profession long enough will eventually be assigned one of *those* kids. A teacher who is willing to be innovative and to master these tools can instill hope, the promise of a life without crime, and one of self-fulfillment, productivity, and integrity. Ms. Sklar's book can help save lives. Her book can help save someone's future.

Centennial, Colorado
May 2015

Addison Adams
Arapahoe County Judge
18th Judicial District

For several years I prosecuted juvenile offenders for crimes ranging from thefts to murder. Most kids I wanted to help get out of the system; very few did I want to really punish. The sight of all these young teenagers in jail uniforms, cuffed hand and ankle, was more than a little heartbreaking. Nearly every case reminded me of how close I once was to being one of them and made me wonder if there was anything that could be done to help them to a different path.

The work of everyone in the courtroom was to help. The judge, the defense attorney, the guardians ad litem, the social workers, the probation officers and me, the prosecutor, all wanted to help, but our contact with and our resources for the kids were so limited I felt helpless. It was and is a good system, perhaps the best that can currently be funded, full of well-meaning people, but it is not nearly enough.

I've never had any doubt that education is the key to giving these troubled kids a chance. If they can learn a little discipline, imagine a little opportunity, and experience a little genuine care, a whole other future could open up for them. But they were so hard to reach. So impossibly hard. Eventually, I gave up and focused on prosecuting adults, which seemed morally simpler—they were grown-ups after all, and I could offer them treatment or prison.

After reading *How Do We Reach Those Kids*, I feel a renewed sense of hope. The ingenious methods Sklar uses to reach out feel so right to this jaded prosecutor. The creativity she advocates and uses has and can help so many. I couldn't help but feel a surge of excitement as I turned the pages. Her passion for saving these kids is as infectious as it is effective.

Centennial, Colorado
May 2015

Clinton McKinzie
Chief Deputy District Attorney, Intake Team
18th Judicial District
Arapahoe County

Mary Sklar is an amazing person. She has taught in mainstream classrooms in America and Russia. But, for the past fourteen years, she has chosen to go where few teachers choose to tread—teaching in a locked, juvenile detention facility. The Marvin W. Foote Youth Services Center is located in the largest judicial district in Colorado. I am a district court judge in that district. I don't hear juvenile cases. What I see are adults charged with serious felonies, some of whom might not have ended up in my courtroom if someone had taken time with them in the way Ms. Sklar suggests.

The situation is serious and immediate. Many kids first become involved in the criminal justice system in a locked juvenile facility, and a disproportionate number of them are minorities. Unless those kids are reached and change their behavior at that time, many become embroiled in a system with little way out. On the outside, our juveniles are being influenced to join a culture of drugs, gangs, and violence. We will continue to watch them end up in adult prisons, victimizing others or becoming victims of crime themselves. The dropout rate and, worse, the who-gives-a-damn attitude deprive them of the one hope they have for a future: an education. This book outlines ideas Ms. Sklar has developed to engage, teach, and reach kids who have no interest in learning or do not see the need for school on the outside. These are kids who are one step away from being written off—and perhaps incarcerated as adults.

Ms. Sklar offers concrete ideas on how to reach and teach those kids—ideas as simple as sitting in a circle rather than classroom rows to give the students a feeling of security, structure, and involvement. Her ideas, however, are just as useful in mainstream classrooms. Her approach gives kids positive reinforcement, better ways to express themselves, and ways to gain feelings of self-worth. I taught eighth grade earth science in an inner-city school many years ago and had trouble with a few students who had little interest in learning and were a distraction to others. I wish I had had Ms. Sklar's book then. I might have continued as a teacher rather than becoming disillusioned and going to law school.

As the old saying goes, "If you always do what you've always done, you will always get the same result." Our current system of educating young people who are about to give up on life is not working. New methods must be attempted to achieve different results. Ironically, I cannot quantify Ms. Sklar's results from where I sit because, if her methods work, I won't see those individuals as adult defendants. Ms. Sklar is convinced her methods work. She sees the results on a daily basis. Ms. Sklar's ideas are not radical; they are practical. They are not difficult; they just require a willingness to try different approaches. They are not expensive; they can be as cheap as rearranging chairs.

If those kids are to have any chance, teachers must explore new and better ways to reach them. We have a nation full of smart, dedicated, and creative teachers. Perhaps some are disillusioned as I was. Perhaps they just need a different compass direction. This book is a good place to start. Our kids—*those* kids—deserve it.

Centennial, Colorado	Christopher C. Cross
May 2015	18th Judicial District Court Judge

1 Helping Kids Reclaim Their Lives

Javontae sauntered into class late, shoulders, neck, and head moving in sync to a silent beat. He sat down and looked up, challenging me to denounce him in any way. He was in charge of the class, and everyone knew it. I welcomed him with a smile.

He had missed the first week of school, and I didn't expect him to be a frequent attendee in the future. Part of me hoped he wouldn't return, as dealing with his attitude would be an ongoing battle of wills. But that was not to be. He started coming to class, sporadically at first, then regularly.

One day I assigned him a paper titled "Hurt People Hurt People," and I asked him to include at least one paragraph that addressed "What I Hate." I told him I'd be in my classroom thirty minutes before school started the next day and would have a coffee waiting for him if he'd care to bring his paper and visit. He was there, waiting for me.

Our conversation started slowly as he haltingly shared his story. He hated school, the system, and life in general. Most of all he hated his dad whom he had repeatedly seen beat his mom or throw her off the walls, usually while high, screaming profanities. Drugs were as common in his home as Cheerios are in mine.

Javontae had started ditching school in the fourth grade, sometimes to protect his mom, sometimes because his life was so chaotic that getting to school simply didn't seem to be on his list of priorities, or because Javontae, on his own, saw no value in school. Attendance counselors would call him periodically and threaten expulsion or even time in a detention center. Their threats and harsh words meant nothing compared to the anger and violence that existed in his own home, and he never felt that anyone at school actually cared if he attended or not.

The choice of school attendance became a moot point the night Javontae savagely beat up his dad after seeing him make sexual advances to his seven-year-old sister. His mom called the police, and Javontae subsequently spent time in a detention center. Now, by court order, he has to attend school at the center wearing an ankle monitor if he wants to avoid another, longer trip to jail.

Amazingly, Javontae doesn't use drugs. He's very bright. He's personable, and he dropped the ghetto strut when he no longer needed it to announce who he was. And he liked our class. When I asked him why, he responded, "It matters."

Like a surprising number of my students, when given the respect and attention they desperately need, Javontae began to value himself and take on assignments that would surprise many who have never given much thought to who *those* kids are in juvenile detention facilities. He became more positive about his future and branched out in his classwork. He chose to memorize "Self Talk," and recite it to the class:

> I'm a person of worth, created by God and given life. I have talents and traits that are unique to me. I can love and be loved. I choose to be loving, to be strong, and to strive every day to be the best that I can be. I could spend my life reacting to what has been, but instead I choose to act. I am capable. I can dream and plan and live out my dream. I will make good choices. If I fail I will learn from my failure and move on with more knowledge than I had before. I choose to rise up and succeed. (Mary Duerksen Sklar)

Javontae described how he had spent his life reacting, and the results hadn't been good ones. He resolved to try acting instead of reacting. He determined to plan his life instead of just letting life happen to him. He began to walk a path that led to success rather than repeated failures. He chose to do what it would take to "rise up and succeed."

He had read *The Hunger Games* by Suzanne Collins and, like millions of teens, loved the book. He asked that a quote from the movie version of that book, "Hope—it is the only thing stronger than fear," be a motto of this class where he had found hope. He became an excellent student in the detention center and subsequently in public school. He has begun to reclaim his life.

≈≈≈

Perhaps the greatest challenge facing America is reclaiming our classrooms just as Javontae has begun to take back his life. Accordingly, it is important that once again American schools become safe places where all students can learn. I want *those* kids—angry, disobedient kids like Javontae—to attend class to learn, not to disrupt; to respect, not to intimidate; to achieve, not to feel shamed. Losing these young people is a tragedy for them; it's a tragedy for

> Love in My Family? Ha!
> All the Stuff told to me.
> I'm Stupid and Unworthy
>
> My life is torn
> Ripped between wanting my family
> And wanting my own future
>
> The lies told to me
> Say two different things
> Am I loved or
> Am I a mistake?
>
> No parents wanting me
> But if one starts they all
> Slip in half.
>
> Step Dad convinced Mom
> Step Mom convinced Dad
> I am some messed up child
> They should not have had.
>
> They say I abused my brothers
> When I was the only one there 'cause
> Our parents did not care.
>
> Adults never believed me
> If they did, they did nothing
> Child abuse in my family
> Goes back years after years
>
> Now comes the time to decide
> Tell the Adults again
> And see if they try.
>   (fifteen-year-old boy)

this country. We need our students to succeed as much as they need us to assist and guide them.

Most of these young people are punished by what goes on in their lives outside of the classroom, whether by neglect, abuse, poverty, lack of adult role models, or any number of other factors that make each day hopeless, scary, depressing, and lonely. Threats, more abuse, and shaming at school only increase the anger those kids already feel and drive them further away from the education that could be their only safe place and provide the possibility of a better future.

Neglected and abused young people are found in every community in this country, regardless of social level or economic means. Too many kids from homes where there is plenty of money are poor in adult attention, supervision, and interaction. When this happens, they go looking for guidance among their peers or older teens, which can lead to gang involvement or clinging to other unguided kids who may or may not provide appropriate leadership. Even in the detention center where I work, many of the young people come from well-to-do families. Kids in need are in need of lots of things; money is pretty far down on the list. Higher up are respect, relationships, and positive role models, to name just a few.

Getting troubled kids to thrive in school is a worthy goal, but how do we accomplish it? We need answers, and we need them quickly. Right now we are losing kids by the thousands—good and poor students alike.

I teach institutionalized kids who are being given a last chance. I've had the pleasure of developing principles and techniques that have helped students, teachers, and schools succeed. They don't cost taxpayer dollars or require legislation. They don't demonize teachers or parents. The ideas and procedures are laid out clearly in this short book. They will make a difference. Teachers, parents, administrators, parent-teacher organizations, and concerned citizens can all have a part in helping our students and our schools be victorious in this battle to reach and teach our students—*those* kids.

If students who have given up, who have no hope, whose relationship with school seems beyond repair, can be turned around—and I've seen it happen more times than I can count—then common sense would tell us that we cannot afford to waste another day.

2 Lost in Society, Lost in School

American schools today have to strive against conditions uncommon in many parts of the world where public education is succeeding. In our society, educators are challenged to get the attention of kids who are captivated by titillating media, savage video games, gang associations, rap music, drug experimentation, and life on the streets. The excitement of these influences is hard to replicate or compete with in a classroom.

Schools are expected to inspire kids who come to us from a society that in large part rejects or only pays lip service to the values that used to help bring order to the classroom. Do well in school. Education is the key to your future. Study hard to be somebody. Respect your teacher. If mores like these once again became the norm, our young people would be learning more and attending school more often. However, teachers must deal with attitudes as they are now.

Parents from other countries don't understand the culture in many of our schools. One distressed mother asked me why we spend so much time at the beginning of each school year reviewing what the students had learned the year before: "Do they think my child is stupid? Why this waste of time when they should be learning new things?" Other parents are anguished by our culture of celebrity. One parent expressed it this way: "My son and daughter always wanted to look good before they came here, but in America looking good is more important than anything else. If I won't buy them a pair of *J*s they're embarrassed to go to school. I didn't even know what *J*s were. Now I understand they're a brand of shoes called Air Jordans, and they cost more than one hundred dollars. That's the entire sum I send overseas to help my family each month to help them stay alive. Shoes or life—that is the choice I have to make for my kids to go to school here. How is it that my kids are so afraid of the ridicule they've gotten that they actually want me to sacrifice family for shoes?"

Students entering American schools also bring concerns. I have a friend whose new stepdaughter, Natasha, was raised in Belarus. When she moved to the United States, she was thirteen years old. She was raised by her mother, who did her best to see that she was well educated even though they had little money. In Belarus, she went to public school and became an accomplished violinist.

Natasha had many questions about school when she arrived in the United States, but what were most telling were her questions about attendance and homework: "Will I be kicked out of school if I get sick and miss days? Will I not be allowed to continue in school if I am unable to complete my homework assignments?" Her biggest concern about America was not being allowed to stay in school. She knew that school was the most important thing she had to do.

Because we cannot change the environment our students come from, our sphere of influence is our students in the classroom. As a teacher, I believe it is incumbent on me to demonstrate the value and relevance of education to the students' personal lives. A young person who can envision a future where education has given him options will be more apt to attend school and try to learn rather than choosing to disrupt and ditch. If we can get the message that school attendance is essential to success across to students, we will have more students who, like Natasha, put showing up and completing homework at the top of their priority lists.

Frequently, students who are not succeeding are absent, ditching school many days of the year. In my classroom at the detention facility, I have had many students, ages sixteen to eighteen, who have less than one semester of high school credit. Frankly, many of them don't care. What they do on the streets is more exciting and pays better than the usual day jobs they hear about.

Additionally, many students transfer from one school to another too often to maintain any educational continuity. It is an unintended consequence of the mobility that is common in our society. Families that don't value education, or whose financial situation is tenuous, are quicker to move their kids many times during a school year. Again, our sphere of influence is our students. If our relationship with the student allows us to make contact with a parent, we have a chance to increase the attachment to the school to include both parent and student. If a parent feels welcome in the school, our influence grows, increasing the chances that the student will feel more committed to coming to class. With greater attachment to the school, perhaps parents will make a greater effort to see that kids attend school and avoid excessive transfers from school to school.

Tragically, many students come from fragile homes and communities where young people have no mentors who value education, where kids don't even feel safe, supported, or encouraged. Varying segments of American society have norms that cause or allow varying outcomes in the educational success of their young people. The affluence in some areas of the United States has, in some cases, taken away much of the drive to excel that exists in numerous developing nations. In other communities, the norms of attending school every day, studying hard to make As, and determining to graduate from high school or beyond are not prevalent. In many American communities, the concepts of taking advanced or very difficult classes or of working with tutors or doing additional studies until late in the night are rare, although common in some parts of the world.

I conducted a workshop for teachers in Holeta, Ethiopia. Classes for these teachers often consisted of sixty or more students. I asked what a teacher would do if a student became disruptive. There was silence after which I was told that if this were to happen, the child would be sent away. Their silence told me more than their words. Their students know that they must get an education if they want to succeed and live at a higher economic level than their parents. The consequences of being sent away were grave and almost unthinkable to teachers and students alike.

Inasmuch as our schools and teachers cannot alter the after-school environments of our students, they can and must find ways to reach and inspire any and all students who walk into their classrooms. However difficult it may be, it is our calling, and we can make a difference in the world by doing so.

This challenge very often feels beyond our ability to handle. James was a student who came to trust me enough that he told me his story—a story that is only one of many that I

> **Take a Walk in My Dreams!**
>
> Take a walk in my dreams
> And see what goes through my mind
> A lot of things that I've hidden
> That not another soul will find
> So many things that hurt real deep
> Just trying to find my fame
> Scars split open and never shut
> From suffering so much pain
> Looking down the barrel of guns
> From enemies I can't see
> Feeling real pain and hearing the screams
> As if this weren't a dream
> Now dressed in all black & waiting to see
> Something known as tragic
> I walked right up and stood my ground
> Putting flowers in the basket
> Suddenly as something shook
> I just recalled what happened
> All it took was just one look
> It was me inside that casket
> Everybody lives rough lives
> Well, that's what it seems
> Warning comes before destruction
> Listen to Your Dreams!
>   (seventeen-year-old boy)

had to steel myself against in order to help James and others like him overcome horrendous home experiences and begin to take charge of their own lives. He described how he spent his after-school hours for slightly more than three years. He and his siblings were to go immediately home and to their rooms where they sat on their beds. James said they were not allowed to move, for any reason, until dinner, and then they were sent immediately to bed.

I thought perhaps James was exaggerating and asked what if they had to go to the bathroom. He reiterated that they had to stay on their beds and that their dad made regular rounds to be sure they had not moved. If they did move, he would take a pan of hot grease he kept on the burner and pour grease slowly down their backs. I said something such as, "Please, James, your dad would burn you if you had to go to the bathroom?" He didn't say a word but slowly stood, turned his back to me, and pulled up his shirt. His back was covered with long, raised scars—the ugly evidence of the monstrous torture of a child.

This is a book of tools, a book of *doing*. It is not filled with educational theories. We can use these tools to develop the skills and relationships in our classrooms that will allow *those* kids to stay in the classroom where they have the best chance of earning an education that will provide a solid foundation for their future.

3 Relevance Ignites Energy in the Classroom

Young people who grow up experimenting with drugs, playing violent video games, watching tasteless or X-rated movies, hanging out on the streets, making gang affiliations, living in families that rarely eat dinner or talk together, may shock you with what they do and do not know. In schools, I've heard the following: "Did Hitler have a last name?" "Didn't Maine used to be a country?" "Does Japan smell like rice?" "Sure I know about Egypt and China. In China they pull each other around in carts and in Egypt they wear towels on their heads. So what's to know?" Soon my generation will pass the baton of leadership to *those* kids. Will they be able to lead America? Will they be able to help America compete in the world?

Recently, in an American public school, I asked the students to name the man who lived in another country during the late 1800s and early 1900s, was a leader of his people, and instrumental in ending British colonization. The students had no idea whom I was talking about. Just in case they had seen the brilliant movie with Ben Kingsley portraying Gandhi's life, I mentioned that he dressed in the style of an Indian peasant and was emaciated due to numerous hunger strikes. Finally, one student proudly waved his hand, confident of his reply. His answer was "Aladdin." No one laughed. How can schools in America have fallen this low?

So the pivotal questions are: How do we raise the standard of education in America? How do we hold students' interest long enough to teach them what they so desperately need to know? How do we encourage young people to make class attendance a priority? If students are living in trauma outside of school, how can we make education have relevance in their lives?

How do we find answers to the four questions above? We probably won't find them in theory-of-education textbooks or technological advances and probably not in stricter or more relaxed disciplinary approaches. We've tried spending more and more money; we blame parents, teachers, or administrators. However, I know of no union, no standardized testing, and no program dictated by politicians or others that have significantly helped students perform better academically.

We find the necessary skills to teach kids well, and differently, within us and within our experience. It is our courageous imagination and our determined belief in the possibility of youth that draws us into the teaching profession. If our passion for teaching has been stifled by disappointments, lack of collegial support, lack of student appreciation, aggressive or threatening teen behaviors, or sparse acknowledgment of a job well done, there is still reason to continue.

If we can remember what it felt like when we first wanted to teach, that fresh perspective and love for the career and the students, we have a place to begin. We can take back the classroom with renewed energy and enthusiasm. With an approach that puts respect first, respect for learning and for everyone in the classroom including the teacher, the days can take on fresh meaning. With new tools to add to the adventure, who could do it better? We have experience. We've been there. We know what it's like in the depths of the trenches. We know how great the need is, and we absolutely can help a young person reclaim his life. The one essential to achievement in the classroom is a teacher who is committed to inspiring each student to want to learn.

The teacher is the answer to raising the standard of American education. The more fully we embrace our unique talents and courageously reveal ourselves to the students, the more successful we will be. Kids just want the truth, but truth that is relevant to their lives. Being real can be scary, but it is also fun, and the more we practice it the more confident we will become. Our success will encourage greater freedom to try new things and to help the students dare what they never imagined they could attempt.

※

I was blessed to be reared in a nurturing midwestern community where the language of my home and neighborhood was gentle and the discipline was mild. The family involvement in my life at every turn was comforting and constant. This background turned out a pretty corny grown woman whose language is fairly bland compared to that of most of my students, and my experiences, although I have travelled a lot, have been tame compared to those of most of the students who come into my classroom. I don't tolerate or use bad language, and my students know it; at first they think I'm kidding because it is so much a part of their lives, but once they understand that I am serious about elevating the level of discourse in my classroom,

---

Ms. Sklar, I just thought I would write and tell you how your class made a difference in my life. You opened my eyes to the world, showed me I could be someone, and showed me how essential goal setting is. Which in turn has helped me a lot and I appreciate you a lot.

I was going down a pretty miserable path, which could only end in a dead end. Now I am finished with school and have been drug and alcohol free for over a year and 4 months. If you can live that way, without drugs-and you don't even eat candy and live an absolutely wonderful life, so can I.

I know the difference between school and life: In school you are given a lesson then given a test. In life you are given a test that leads you and teaches you a lesson. I'm glad I had you there to help me through my lesson.

Thank you.

(successful graduate of the detention center)

they begin to appreciate their "corny" teacher. They are quick to put new students on notice that coarse language is not allowed in Ms. Sklar's class, and they help remind each other. We will see later in this book a creative way to deal with foul talk.

I never stand in front of the class and simply lecture. I know from experience that I have to keep moving. I have to change the tone of my voice; I may speak nearly in a shout if the subject matter requires it, and I may whisper—it always gets their full attention. I may turn my back to them. I may stand on a chair to make a point. I often play music, speak in rhymes, or clap. Sounds are powerful. Nothing is more deadly in a classroom than boredom, especially with kids who are burned-out, so I never give them a chance to yawn.

I ask kids if I can use them in playacting examples of kindness, or meanness, courage, or fearfulness, or anything that draws them into a class interaction. A kid may laugh or refuse, but eventually, as some see my all-in behavior, the kids will begin to participate because they see that it is safe and can even be fun. If I am not afraid to take chances in front of them—be a little weird—and try things that seem strange, perhaps they can do it too.

I have a friend who took a two-year leave of absence from a high-paying job to teach in an inner-city high school. A captivating speaker and knowledgeable in his subject area, he was someone young people thought was a very cool guy. The first day of school he was ready, enthusiastically awaiting the kids for his first class. More than twenty were enrolled. He waited in the hall by his door. Three kids came in and sat down—no one else. The halls were filled with teens laughing and having a great time. He began to search for his students, asking for them by name, trying to create some organization out of the hall chaos. Fifteen minutes after school was to begin an assistant dean told him to go into his class and get it started. The administrator speculated that directing the kids in the halls might provoke a confrontation or even a fight.

The next day a few more kids showed up for class, but by the end of the week he still had fewer than ten students. He considered asking if he could literally teach in the halls. He believed in his gut that the kids would be intrigued by what they learned if he could just have a chance with them. Without seeking permission, he began teaching in the hall. He would apologize later if he were breaking too many rules. He taught in the hall for the next week and then moved back into his classroom, not with ten students but with more than thirty—the maximum number that could fit.

He had the right skills within him to reach kids. He was passionately devoted to reaching out and connecting, but the system, bound in fear and the safety of following the rules, could have prevented him from teaching *those* kids. I have no idea what he did in the hall or how he did it, but I am sure that what he did was different, and it worked.

We need access to the kids, and it does not need to be in traditional venues or styles. Whatever it takes, whatever the curriculum area, whatever the administrative doctrine, we must get the kids into class, at least for a try. This is step one.

Then we must ask ourselves how we can make what we teach relevant to our students' lives, and how the subject matter can be broadened to develop relationships between teachers and students and between student and student. We must release any fear of the students laughing at our efforts. Whatever we try, if it's an honest effort to connect, the students will be accepting. They may laugh, but it's with affection and, frankly, appreciation, knowing that we care about them and about what we're all learning.

There may only be a few chances to grab their attention. Teachers must go for it! If it's edgy, it may work. If they feel our passion, it may inspire them. We must be willing to take risks, reach out, imagine something, share a story, be extreme, be loud, be quiet, be fast, slow down, be fully there with the students we get to teach. Relevance to their lives is the key to sustaining their interest and insuring that learning stays with them when they walk out of the classroom. Here's an example.

I was teaching a class where fewer than half of the students knew the word Holocaust. *Those* kids might very well sabotage any learning that could take place if we merely opened our textbooks to study a chapter titled "Holocaust" or if they were to use an online program where they could try to get the facts to pass a test. I wanted the kids to learn the facts, but also to understand and care deeply about the tragedy and to apply the significant lessons of the Holocaust to their own personal code of behavior choices.

After reflection, I remembered a scene from the movie *Freedom Writers*. This powerful film is based on a nonfiction book, *The Freedom Writers Diary*, a 1999 portrayal of an idealistic but determined teacher at Woodrow Wilson High School in Long Beach, California. The author, Erin Gruwell, did what it took to reach *those* kids. She formed relationships and found avenues to make education relevant to the lives of her students. In the film, she makes a comparison between gangs in Los Angeles and the Nazis, the biggest gang of them all. It's a dramatic, powerful scene in which her students realize they can identify with the frightening, powerless position of the Jews when the Nazis were in power in Germany.

Before I asked the students to read or study one fact concerning the Holocaust, I showed that eight-minute film clip from *Freedom Writers*. The kids were captivated. The Holocaust became meaningful to them, just as it had to the students at Woodrow Wilson High. They watched, they could relate, and from that moment on, learning about the Holocaust was a powerful and relevant experience for each of those students.

They related it to a quote by Edmund Burke painted on the classroom wall: "The only thing necessary for the triumph of evil is for good men to do nothing." They searched their souls: Would I have hidden a Jew in my attic? Would I have faced the truth and done something about the pogroms? The students also extended the discussion to issues in their lives today: "Sometimes I don't even let uncool kids sit with me at lunch. I'm going to change that." "I saw a kid jumped into a gang last week. He was crying, and I didn't help him. It never even occurred to me. I'm disgusted with myself." Every student could apply the lessons of the Holocaust to his life. The unit was a success, and the students knew they would live better lives because of what they had learned.

It is not always easy to find these hooks, but it is worth the effort. Taking the time to explore nontraditional or unexpected ways to present material always pays off. Doing this brings historical events and lasting educational memories into the classroom and into the lives of students. This relevancy approach encourages students to ask questions, think about what they've learned in class, and grow from the experience.

4 Relationships

As we know, many young people today come from broken homes; some of them are *really* broken. The terms broken home or dysfunctional family are used pretty casually to refer to families where there has been a divorce or where there has been significant discord between family members; however, the students I see often are themselves broken by the extreme circumstances they have endured in their homes and communities.

I have been astonished by the number of students I've met who either don't know dad, hate dad because they've seen him abuse his family members, or have a dad in prison. It is not unusual for them to have uncles, aunts, siblings, and other family members in prison as well. I will never forget the day I was filling in for another teacher. Each student was doing independent, online research. All of a sudden a girl screamed, "There's my daddy!" She had been searching prison websites looking for her father, whom she had never met. There was his mug shot in front of her, and she was sobbing with joy to have finally seen his face.

I've found that the mother or grandmother is often the only parental figure for many young people. Mom may be a hardworking woman, trying her best to take care of her kids, or mom may be high most of the time, leaving her children to fend for themselves. How do we reach kids who come to us from such fragile foundations?

Our schools must become places of belonging in addition to places of learning. Many may say this is not our responsibility, but will a student learn and achieve, will he even want to be in school if his home life is in chaos and the school, perhaps large and unfamiliar to him, doesn't feel welcoming?

How can teachers who are overburdened with state-mandated responsibilities and curriculum demands possibly add personal responsibility for building relationships to an already packed schedule? Can we keep asking more of them? How can an administrator provide the leadership for the school's role in opening its doors to every child and parent? Impossible, many would say. Laughable.

But let's take a step back and look at priorities. If our goal is to create an environment in which learning can take place, we have no choice but to put relationships first. The time spent forming teacher-student bonds lays the groundwork for a classroom that has a chance of being a setting where kids can learn. If the classroom is the one place where an effort is made to make each person feel important, welcome, and respected, the first battle—keeping kids in school—is on the way to being won. Imagine what a difference it would make if these relationships become the key influences that motivate these kids to work for and to seek an education.

Just this morning I was visiting with a fifteen-year-old student who lived with his mother, a drug addict, until he was five, at which time he moved in with his grandmother. She's a good woman, but leaves for work at 5:30 a.m., six days a week. This young man has had to get himself up and to school all on his own since elementary school. Support, security, and mentoring are nonexistent for him. The resulting isolation made him vulnerable. As his family became increasingly fractured, other interested parties stepped in and filled the void in his life. It's no surprise that by the time he was fifteen he had made some bad choices and is now in serious trouble.

A gang has become his family. He's given up on what most would call a decent life. Nothing has worked for him, and he's about made the decision to live on the streets. He can make more money by hustling and selling drugs than he will ever make with a respectable job, even if we know he'll lose it all and probably his life in the tragic process. I'm trying to encourage him to consider other options, but how can I make the sale?

One possibility to help this young man, and many other young people as well, would be for him to belong somewhere that's supportive and positive. This is essential in the absence of a functioning family. Schools in America, in addition to educating students, must provide places of belonging to prevent this young man, and millions like him, from becoming one of *those* kids.

I lived in Russia where I worked as a volunteer teacher in a public school. I learned so much from this experience. I hope I was helpful to them in the challenging times at the end of their communist era. I brought some ideas from American schools, but I took away other concepts that changed many of my beliefs about helping kids succeed.

A significant concept to which I was introduced in Russia was that the same school educated young people from first grade through graduation after grade eleven. It seemed to me that schools couldn't adequately teach and provide for such a broad age span. Although I initially opposed this idea of teaching all grades under one roof, I came to see it as a wonderful system for very specific reasons. Kids grow up there; it was their second home. Kids belong. Teachers know the students, their siblings, and their parents. They work and study in relationship with one another. If

---

The Ws of Life

Who is mine to call my own?
Mom or dad, "f'd" up and alone.
What's mine to call my own?
Needles, weed, a stolen phone.
Where's a home to call my own?
I prefer to hang out in a homeless zone.
When will life change, will there be pride to own?
Maybe, but not what another might clone.
Why is this the life I own?
Started at birth and It's all I've known.

(sixteen-year-old boy)

a student's behavior began to change from positive to negative, the teachers noticed more quickly, much as they would with their own family members or neighbors. There is a connection that's been developed over time. Teachers know the kids and the families well enough to call them, to intervene early, and to make changes deemed necessary, often saving the child. The student success I saw defied all my expectations. I experienced the impact of long-term, significant relationships and a sense of belonging.

Another benefit of one school for students of all ages and grades is mentorship. Older kids in this same school routinely tutored younger kids and, in the process, a mentoring relationship developed. This is mutually beneficial. Both feel cared for, important, productive, and have someone with whom they relate. This individualized tutoring-mentoring relationship raises academic performance for both the tutor and the younger one being tutored. The tutor needs to truly understand the subject in order to teach it, and the other benefits from individualized instruction. Academic performance is enhanced and relationships are created. Students belong and students learn.

American schools tend to be quite large and, some students would say, intimidating. Furthermore, our students' educational careers are usually broken into elementary, middle and high school—three institutions rather than one. If a family relocates one or more times during these years, the educational disruption is even greater. I suggest minimizing the interruptions. I suggest we consider a one-school plan. Assuming the present divorce rate continues, as well as the mobility of friends, neighbors, and others who could symbolize security and significance to young people, perhaps initiating this one-school option will add the sense of belonging that will help our young thrive and succeed. I know this is controversial, but I've seen it work and know there are many advantages.

At a time in our nation when families are less intact and more mobile than in previous years, I suggest our schools consider closing ranks and facilitating closer relationships between teachers, students, and their families. Variations of this one-school approach already exist in the United States. Some districts have two schools, upper and lower grades, on one campus and both share the library, gym, and cafeteria. Some have one school for all grades, and the multipurpose areas, like those listed above, are separate buildings but within one campus.

Let's get this idea into public discourse and see if it can become a widespread reality. Let's see what the results are. Initially, I bet it will mean less truancy due to a sense of belonging and greater learning as individualized tutoring becomes a part of daily life at school. Fresh ideas will energize the discussion as we address the challenges we face in educating kids whose lives are fractured and in need of old-fashioned adult involvement and concern.

The fifteen-year-old boy, who has been getting himself to school since he was five, has tried to make it out there all alone. He has not succeeded. He will be a father in three months, and he's on his way to prison.

5 Respectful Interactions

The importance of relationships cannot be overstated. Relationships foster a sense of connection, which encourages attendance, and, in turn, promotes increased learning. It is not helpful or appropriate for there to be a buddy relationship between teacher and student or to have an environment where kids come to class and chill with their homies. Building relationships that set the right tone for spirited give-and-take in the classroom does not suggest an attitude of familiarity.

Teachers who need students to be their friends will be unable to draw appropriate boundaries or create the respect that is critical for students to thrive and achieve. Trust, consistency, and respect are the bases for suitable, effective relationships. The best teachers will establish a mentor-like association. The teacher is certified, comes to the classroom with verifiable competence, signifies authority, demonstrates capability, and is worthy of respect. Therefore, the classroom, while interesting and engaging, is not a party. Students walk in to learn; they do not dance or strut into the room. The key word will be respect—for learning, for knowledge, for fellow students, for the teacher, and for self. The atmosphere will become charged with an excitement for learning that will transcend any lesser group dynamic.

We as teachers know what respect is, and we want respectful interactions, but how do we achieve them? I stand at the door and welcome students as they come into class. I make eye contact, and I smile. I try to bring up something from a previous conversation: "I hope your grandma's feeling better." "Love the haircut." "I can't believe you're back! I'm delighted to see you." "I hope you're ready for class today; it's going to be crazy." Connections begin at the threshold of the classroom. If something is already going on inside the classroom, students are more likely to be drawn in even before everyone has settled into his seat. Perhaps there is music playing or a provocative statement on the board or a poignant video clip playing. A personal greeting combined with a classroom that is already energized for learning and interaction sets the tone. Such a setting encourages the students to join in, leaving behind those few who might consider disrupting the class. They will catch up; it rarely fails.

Suppose a student is talking to another student or not paying attention or not respecting class expectations. I might ask, "Excuse me, am I interrupting?" I smile and hold that smile, the first time. I always recognize in some way or call attention to any behavior problems that occur. I go to the problem; I do not ignore it. I may stroll over to the students where there's a hiccup and sit between them or stand beside them, perhaps in total silence for a moment until the kids involved react and quiet themselves.

But suppose they don't. I may stand in silence quite close to them, or I may ask if there was something they wanted to say or something they wanted to share. I am fully present near them; my body conveys a relaxed, in-charge demeanor. Body language can be key. I take a wider stance, a calm presentation, again with eye contact, and a deadly serious look or a smile. It's human nature to talk faster and become somewhat jerky in our movements when we get nervous. Kids pick up on this, and the teacher loses power. When tensions rise, I slow down my speech, my movements, and my gestures. Slowing down, even to a stop, is more powerful than anything hurried. Doing the unexpected always gets a reaction from the kids. The other kids will love it, and often peer pressure is my best means of support.

I ask lots of questions about life, opinions about a topic we're studying, or something happening in the world. If the kids talk more than I do, I've succeeded. If students are engrossed in conversation and feel they are being heard, they are more likely to pay attention and care about contributing. Boredom is the enemy. Engagement is the goal.

As I assume a leadership presence in the classroom, I can better relate to all of the students. Unsure kids feel safer if I display power, and disruptive students seem to respect me more because of it. It's an old theory that kids need boundaries, but *those* kids are the prime example of ones who need to know how to rein themselves in. Most of them have lived in fear their entire lives: fear of abusive parents, fear of gang leaders, fear of the unknown dangers around the corner, fear of being asked to do things they are afraid to do by people they perceive as more powerful than they are. Fearful kids bluff; the attitude they put on is meant to scare the average teacher. But when I find the courage to take a stand and show them I am up to the challenge of caring about who they are and what they will become, I am energized. From this position, I can reach out and make a difference in the lives of those kids who may never give school another chance if I lose them.

> The first day [I was in your class] you told me that I was smart and how you hoped I was gonna change my life. Well you have no idea how much that touched me, and what it meant....To be honest I think you, some relatively random person in my life, told me that I could really do something with my life, actually made me change. I believe your words were really what gave me my final push to change my life. And for that I'll always be grateful....I love quotes and one of my favorite ones is, "Destiny is not a chance. Destiny is a choice."
>
> Thank you Ms., you really helped me. Thanks for your kindness and generosity...when very few people even cared.
>
> (seventeen-year-old boy)

Kids who have been disappointed, betrayed, or dismissed in the past are on the alert for signs that the teacher is just like all the others. They are wounded and scared. I must show compassion, strength, and kindness, but no fear or hesitation. They need to trust in me to lead the way on this adventure.

6 Unique Classrooms

I am constantly thinking of ways I can make my classroom different from all the other classes kids might have experienced. How can I give mine a unique personality? I ask myself, what would make kids want to come in and stay awhile?

One of my classrooms is room 101. Kids tell me that when they first entered the room, they thought the class might be interesting; some have used the word intriguing. What did they see? They immediately came across certificates, awards, and multiple lists of kids' names who had accomplished something. They tell me it felt as if "This class isn't boring" or "Hmmm...A lot of kids have done okay here." Many said they thought perhaps they, too, could experience approval and achievement, not failure and humiliation or shame. I do write kids' names on the board—when they're doing well.

Positive words and quotes are painted right on the walls of my classroom. They include such words and concepts as Respect, Failure Is for Learning, and Life Is Choices. Encouraging, challenging statements, used as responses to roll call, are written on the board. Strange things are hanging from the ceiling: an eight-foot S and a two-foot K.

The S stands for the stupidity in the world. When a student does some great learning, he can tear off a piece of the Styrofoam S because he has reduced the stupidity in the world. (Obviously, the wording is important. The stupidity is in the world, not in the students.) The smaller K represents the knowledge in the world. When a student shows that he has learned something of significance, he can add segments to the K, visually depicting the growing body of knowledge in the world.

The kids I teach are very worldly and streetwise. They know words I didn't hear until long after I was an adult with children, and they tease me because they think much of what I do in the classroom is corny. I have strict rules about what language is acceptable and what behavior is appropriate. But these young people who come into my classroom, rough edges and all, beam like choir boys when they are allowed to add segments to the *K* that represents knowledge or symbolically reduce the stupidity in the world by tearing pieces from the *S*. One year, students kept the pieces of stupidity they had torn off. They became trophies, and I printed off a congratulatory statement they kept with the broken-off Styrofoam. It was interesting to see just how much this meant.

Dozens of large photographs depicting people and lifestyle alternatives around the world are hanging on the walls. Shelves of books, for kids to borrow or take, line one wall. My friends have been generous book donors.

Music from a variety of cultures might be playing, or an excerpt from a movie, news clip, or speech might be streaming via my Apple TV as the students enter the room. One day, freshly mown grass was on the floor, and Ethiopian coffee and popcorn were being served while we were studying eastern Africa.

> I like coming to class, every day. It has had a big impact on my life. Every day is different in some way, but in another way it's not. I know that I will be welcomed and respected no matter what. I've learned that there are so many people in the world who are much worse off than I am. We have learned that no matter what the situation or what you have been through you can come out of it as a stronger person.
>
> The two words I use for our class are caring and innovative. I learn something every day. In fact most often Ms Sklar asks each of us, "What did you learn today?" We always have an answer to that. Lastly Ms Sklar has impacted my life by helping me realize that I am a person of worth & that is one thing in my life that I can truly say will never leave the forefront of my thoughts.
>
> (sixteen-year-old girl)

Other subjects can be presented in intriguing ways. One excellent math teacher celebrated "Pie" Day every year. The number pi, 3.14159, is a mathematical constant. The teacher arranged a competition to see which students could extend pi out the farthest. The winners got to throw cream pies at a volunteer administrator and herself on the playground after school. The kids lined up to watch and roared their approval for both the adults and the winning students.

There can be something to capture the interest of just about everyone in the classroom. We can help increase positive interaction and expectations among students who are otherwise reluctant to give school another chance. As apathy decreases and barriers to learning fall, academic performance improves.

7 Classroom Seating

A classroom needs to be a place of belonging. It needs to have its own flavor. It must be inviting, unique, safe, and close. I think kids who have experienced trauma or have spent time on the streets need to sit facing one another in a circle, or sometimes a *U* shape, so everyone can see everyone else. Often these kids are nervous about who might be behind them and what that unseen person might be doing. I, too, sit in the circle, but my back is to the door so that only I could be surprised by what happens there. The first time she came to class, one student told me she felt safer than she has ever felt in a classroom. Usually, she goes straight to the back row and sits there. She doesn't know what kids may be saying or doing behind her if she doesn't claim that back-row seat. "I don't want to be the victim of a surprise attack," she stated.

Why Mom?

Although it was long ago
    It feels like yesterday
And you were here with me
    But then everything changed
What am I supposed to do
    without a mom like you?
Just sit here in solitude?
    It's like I never knew you

You never took the time to love me,
You never took the time to understand.
    This isn't what I wanted to be
        a boy in misery.
Why can't you understand my pain?
How can I explain?

You never took the time to love me,
You never took the time to understand
    A memory is all I'll ever have
Because of you I'm just
    a lonely boy.

                (sixteen-year-old boy)

One of my students came to my classroom full of swagger and fear. Eventually, he told me his story: "When I was younger, my mom and dad would fight every night. I was scared. They would always put me in the middle of their arguments. I never knew what to do. My parents finalized their divorce in April and told me to choose where I wanted to live. It was hard because I didn't want either of them to be mad at me, but I chose to stay with my mom because my dad is more dangerous. Now I'm afraid he'll catch me on the way to school." This boy would have been unable to sit with his back to the door of the classroom. He asked for my help and my protection; the visceral fear he lived with daily made school attendance nearly impossible even in a prison school where he was behind locked doors.

Once a classroom is safe and once students feel safe, kids can begin to focus on the curriculum. This closed circle, in addition to feeling safe to kids, creates a sense of belonging. It becomes our group, our club, our team, but one that is welcoming. When a new student arrives, those in the circle become the hosts. I ask the kids who have been there to tell the newcomer what's important about our class. Usually, they talk about respect, and they often explain that they sit in a circle because everyone is equal, which makes the class a positive experience. Sometimes there may be gang-related tensions but those are put aside in our class, and every student knows that respect wins over any other classification—be it gang A, gang B, or no gang; nerd or cool; good student or poor student. It is our class, our circle, our hour to learn.

Occasionally, a student may be in a really bad headspace and sit back from the circle. I merely say that we need him or her and that we need each other. A student pulling back from our group is alone, and we all lose by his absence. These students often struggle to find a way to connect when contact with others has primarily brought pain and conflict in their lives. Surprisingly,

John Donne's poem "No Man Is an Island" is a favorite of some of my most rough-edged kids.

Being needed provides powerful motivation to come to class and participate. Kids who believe they have a role to play are kids who contribute. They realize they have a responsibility to keep our class moving and intact.

An exception to sitting in a circle with kids facing each other may be used out of respect for students affected by ADHD. One of my sons had ADHD and needed to sit close to the front of classrooms where there would be fewer visual distractions between him and the teacher. This need could be accommodated by a U-shaped seating plan.

Although I want to close my classroom for a sense of safety and belonging, I also want to open it wide for us to experience the heritage, history, excitement, knowledge, and ideas from all over the world and beyond that are waiting for us to discover.

Into our group we welcome guest speakers, film, those who have been to places and experienced life in ways that will enrich our group and create excitement about possibilities that exist for every student. Dreams are born and plans are created right from our circle of student belonging.

8 Roll Response

In room 101 every minute is valuable, and we don't waste time calling the roll with the kids responding "Here" or "Present." Rather, we answer with a phrase, a sentence, or a quote I write on the board; I write a new response each month. I have two reasons for doing this. First, due to the fact that kids come into my classroom from a variety of backgrounds, grade levels, and school-attendance patterns, written roll responses provide a quick appraisal of a student's reading ability. Second, the quotes bring into our classroom ideas that provide immediate food for conversation and concepts that make a connection between the world and our lives.

> What was I thinking,
> following the crowd.
> Trying to be cool,
>   Did I actually
>   feel proud?
> They led, I followed, I let
> awful things go,
> I saw, didn't care,
>   The horror,
>   the woe,
> I thought I was right
> To let her be shamed
>   How can I
>   stomach what I
>   did that night?
> (fifteen-year-old boy)

Periodically, we discuss the meaning of the roll responses. The phrases and quotes are great for short writing assignments and are the topic of discussion from time to time throughout the month. Everyone's ideas are heard with respect, and the sense of belonging increases for each student as these conversations continue.

I have been astounded by the interest, even excitement, students show the first day of each month when the new statement is posted. The kids talk about it, compare it with others they may have liked, figure out why I chose it, and suggest ideas for the next month. These quotes seem to waken a longing for substance in the lives of these kids. The following are some of the responses I have used:

- I, (name), understand that every day I make choices, and the result of these choices is my life.
- I, (name), understand that "success is not final, failure is not fatal: it is the courage to continue that counts."—Sir Winston Churchill
- I, (name), understand that "life becomes harder for us when we live for others, but it also becomes richer and happier."—Albert Schweitzer
- I, (name), understand that "although the world is full of suffering, it is also full of the overcoming of it."—Helen Keller
- I, (name), can choose to collect information so that I possess knowledge, and with that knowledge I can become a person of wisdom.
- I, (name), know I have the power and ability to succeed if I make the right choices and have the courage to follow through.
- I, (name), understand that "no one is born a winner or a loser, but everyone is born a chooser."—Keith Davis
- I, (name), understand that "an individual has not started living until he can rise above the narrow confines of his individualistic concerns to the broader concerns of all humanity."—Reverend Martin Luther King Jr.
- I, (name), understand that "one man with courage is a majority."—President Thomas Jefferson
- I, (name), understand that "to say you have no choice is to release yourself from responsibility, and that's not how a person with integrity acts."—Patrick Ness
- I, (name), understand Lincoln's statement: "My great concern is not whether you have failed, but whether you

are content with your failure."—President Abraham Lincoln
- I, (name), understand that "there are darknesses in life and there are lights, and you are one of the lights, the light of all lights."—Bram Stoker
- I, (name), understand that "anyone who never made a mistake has never tried anything new."—Albert Einstein
- I, (name), understand that "a man is but the product of his thoughts. What he thinks, he becomes."—Mahatma Gandhi
- I, (name), understand that self-control is knowing I can, but deciding that I won't.
- I, (name), understand that "life is not a spectator sport. If you're going to spend your whole life in the grandstand just watching what goes on...you're wasting your life."—Jackie Robinson
- I, (name), know that "the man who follows a crowd will never be followed by a crowd."—R. S. Donnell
- I, (name), understand that "our greatest glory is not in never failing, but in getting up every time we fall."—Confucius
- I, (name), learned that "courage was not the absence of fear, but the triumph over it."—President Nelson Mandela
- I, (name), understand that "yesterday is not ours to recover, but tomorrow is ours to win or lose."—President Lyndon Baines Johnson
- I, (name), understand the statement from the movie *The Hunger Games*: "Hope—it is the only thing stronger than fear."—Donald Sutherland, as President Snow
- I, (name), understand Malala's belief that "for a nation to be stable, education must be possible for all people."—Malala Yousafzai

- I, (name), understand the statement: "Do not go where the path may lead, go instead where there is no path and leave a trail."—Ralph Waldo Emerson
- I, (name), understand the statement: "Education is the most powerful weapon you can use to change the world."—President Nelson Mandela
- I, (name), understand the belief that "nothing in the world is more dangerous than sincere ignorance and conscientious stupidity."—Reverend Martin Luther King Jr.
- I, (name), understand that "men are not prisoners of fate, but only prisoners of their own minds."—President Franklin Delano Roosevelt

I was delighted when one day a student said to me, "Miss, I had a crazy dream last night. I dreamed that Winston Churchill came to my house and talked to me about my favorite quote, 'Success is not final, failure's not fatal: it's the courage to continue that counts.' Can you believe I dreamed about Winston Churchill? Hell, Miss, a year ago I'd never even heard of Winston Churchill, and now I'm dreaming about him." How good can it get? *Those* kids are our kids, waiting to grow, to learn, to connect, and to thrive.

9 Quotes Painted on Walls

A student wrote the following to me: "What makes a class interesting is the pride a teacher takes in the class, the 'blood, sweat, and tears' a teacher figuratively sheds each day. If a teacher cares, the students know and will respond in kind. I get really into learning if a teacher listens to my experiences and can connect the subject to my life."

The walls in room 101 are painted with our own version of graffiti, and they seem to make a strong connection with the students. They talk about the quotes, ask about them, and a few kids have even had them tattooed on their bodies—not something I encourage! One day a former student came to the lobby asking to see me; he had a surprise. He turned around and lifted his shirt; there, diagonally across his back, was the quote from Edmund Burke: "The only thing necessary for evil to triumph is for good men to do nothing."

> So we put up a new world map on our wall, and it took several weeks. Students did all the work. I really liked doing it. While the old map was down and we were spackling, we wrote some of our favorite quotes about the world in the bare space. After the new map was up, it was smaller, we decided to make a column of what we call "worldly quotes" next to it. All the kids voted and chose our favorites.
>
> All of us wanted to work on the project. Ms Sklar asked why, and I answered, "It feels good to do something that's going to help some other kids learn." Another kid said, "I like to be chosen to do something. It's nice to feel special, especially when I'm locked up." And, you should see it. The wall looks fine.
>
> (fourteen-year-old boy)

Each wall has one or more quotes painted on it, and the painting was done by the kids. I chose ideas or quotes that I believe are relevant to the students and have the potential to inspire them. I printed each of them onto a plastic transparency sheet. The kids took it from there.

We projected the quotes on the walls, adjusting the projector until the size and location seemed perfect. The students traced the words with Sharpies and then filled in with glossy paint from tubes so the letters wouldn't drip.

Each quote has its own unique font, which kids have noticed and appreciated. Quotes have become an integral and effective part of what happens in our classroom and are a significant aspect of the student buy in that has taken place.

I believe the addition of words, phrases, or quotes to classroom walls increases the interest and relevance of the learning that can take place, regardless of the subject being taught. For example, a math teacher might want to paint Albert Einstein's observation that "pure mathematics is, in its way, the poetry of logical ideas." Einstein also said, "Do not worry about your difficulties in Mathematics. I can assure you mine are still greater." What a boost this gives students who are struggling with math but determined to learn. The "Math Is Radical" bumper sticker is a fun quip that also may energize students in a math classroom.

A computer science teacher might paint these statements from Bill Gates and Steve Jobs, respectively: "Be nice to nerds. Chances are you'll end up working for one." "Be a yardstick of quality. Some people aren't used to an environment where excellence is expected."

A science teacher might choose these from Wernher von Braun and Edward Teller: "Research is what I'm doing when I don't know what I'm doing." "The science of today is the technology of tomorrow."

The choice of quotes that pertains to any subject area is virtually inexhaustible and will be an effective addition to a classroom. The slogans or words give personality to a room. I believe that the increased interest shown in the quotes will heighten the relevance of curriculum to personal lives. The discussions of the quotes are key to developing relationships in the classroom and help us do a better job as we try to reach and teach *those* kids.

The following pages will include commentaries on the eight quotes I chose for the walls of room 101.

- RESPECT
- KNOWLEDGE IS POWER.
- WHEN MY PRIORITIES CHANGED, MY BEHAVIORS FOLLOWED.
- LIFE IS CHOICES.
- FAILURE IS FOR LEARNING.
- IT IS IMPOSSIBLE FOR A MAN TO LEARN WHAT HE THINKS HE ALREADY KNOWS.
- SUCCESS IS ATTITUDE. ATTITUDE IS 10 PERCENT WHAT HAPPENS TO YOU AND 90 PERCENT HOW YOU RESPOND.
- THE ONLY THING NECESSARY FOR THE TRIUMPH OF EVIL IS FOR GOOD MEN TO DO NOTHING.

My students have followed the young Pakistani girl, who was the recent recipient of the Nobel Peace Prize, Malala Yousafzai, as she has courageously spoken out for the right of all people to gain an education. The students want to add to the wall these powerful words from Malala's address to the United Nations: "One child, one teacher, one book, one pen can change the world."

I said at the beginning that we became graffiti artists, and I meant this in the most positive way. Nothing in my classroom has been achieved with more care and dedication. The students took great pride in doing their best work. They feel constantly surrounded by words that express how many of them want to live their lives in the future.

One of my students, Ramon, grew up fighting. He was big, and he definitely knew how to fight. He had learned from his dad. Ramon's father liked beating up his wife and his kids. As the eldest son, Ramon was a fighter by the fifth grade. He would fight his dad when his dad hit his mother or his siblings. But Ramon didn't fight casually; he fought with a palpable rage. Consequently, he didn't know when or how to stop. One time he hurt his dad badly, and when his dad went to the hospital, Ramon went to jail.

> Love is something you always have.
> Love is something you always learn to give.
> Life is something you are given.
> Life is what you live.
> Respect is what I have never had.
> Can you feel it and forgive?
> Breathing, crying, screaming, laughing, smiling is who you are.
> Take who you are and work for who you want to be.
> (fifteen-year-old boy)

When I met this thirteen-year-old boy, he could read at the fourth-grade level and had few other academic skills. School didn't matter to him, but taking care of his family did. His rage would erupt with only minuscule provocation. It was a challenge to get him to want to learn, but it was not impossible.

Once he began to experience academic success, he knew, as I did, that he would be much better equipped to take care of his mother and siblings in the future. His dad is now in jail, his mother is receiving shelter and financial assistance, and Ramon will have a diploma the next time he applies for a job. He wrote, "I'm working hard, changing my ways, hoping to be rehabilitated, so I'm the opposite of a sinner."

Ramon's involvement in the project to fill the walls with inspiring quotes was truly a healing experience.

Respect

Ask students why the word *respect* is written in the tallest font of all eight quotes on the classroom walls, and you will hear fervent, opinionated responses. Respect is a hot-button topic for youth today. We probably grew up hearing, "Honor your father and mother." Sadly, many kids today grow up hearing very different messages. "Show some respect. You're my kid, and I can do anything I want with you." "It's my house, and you're stuck. Do what I tell you, or you're out of here for good." "You're a loser/a failure/a worthless piece of shit. Get out, and I don't ever want to see you again."

At the same time, these kids are seeing unspeakable assaults against siblings, mothers, and themselves. They also may live with parents who are addicts or criminals or live in violent, gang-dominated neighborhoods. It is not surprising that they rebel against the unfairness, fear, and desolation of such situations.

The following are typical of what kids say to teachers:

- "If I don't get respect, I don't give respect."
- "When we don't get respect in school, we 'dip' (leave)."
- "Why should I try? I don't get no respect in school."
- "We're put down in school by everyone: kids and teachers. That's one reason we drop out. If there was respect in school, I wouldn't mind going."
- "It's not just me. If my homies don't get respect, we all walk out. We've got better things to do anyhow."

It seems youth culture has no frame of reference for traditional values, including respect for family, elders, our country and the flag, and the worth of school and education. Perhaps this respect has never been modeled for them. Regardless of how or why this estrangement from traditional values has occurred, it comforts students, and me, to know that when respect is valued in the classroom, learning and growth occur.

To initiate a robust discussion, I tell students to reverse the often-repeated phrase, "If I don't get respect, I won't give respect." I ask them to spend a day practicing giving respect *before* they get respect. We share the results the next day. Could they see it as an option that could be a positive change in their lives?

Showing respect has become a standard in room 101. Students frequently remind each other and tell new students that in this class they must remember the *r* word. They like it.

Knowledge is Power.

—Sir Francis Bacon

When young people grow up in an environment where knowledge has little value and where ideas and concepts aren't routinely discussed, school is of little importance and seems to have no relevance to their lives. Disrupting classes and ditching school become reasonable choices. When violence occurs every day in the family and the neighborhood, when drug and gang influences are ever present, young people are understandably more focused on survival than getting an education. These kids may become *those* kids in school.

One day a seventeen-year-old boy said to me, "Miss, I'm ignorant. Can you help me?" His mother was incarcerated when he was born, and he had bounced from foster homes to residential institutions his entire life. We began meeting in my classroom thirty minutes before school began, Monday through Friday. We'd stand in front of the wall-sized map and talk about the world. He would stand in a rather professorial pose, stroking his chin with one hand. One day, as he pondered the world, he asked me, "Miss, is it true you took your family to Ireland over Christmas?" I said, "Yes, I did." He thought for a minute, then asked, "Well, how did you get there?" I replied, "Mike, we flew." "Oh," he responded, looking wisely at the map. "I guess that's better than taking the bus." I tried not to show surprise and asked, "Mike, do you know what all this blue is on the map?" "Yes, I believe it's called ocean." Almost fearfully, I inquired, "Mike, do you know what ocean means?" "It means blue parts on maps, I believe." "Oh, Mike! The blue, the oceans, are water—salt water." "Ah," he said, nodding sagely.

I am constantly in awe of how deprived in every way these children are. Mike had trusted me enough with his fragile ego to tell me he knew he was ignorant. If I had been careless with that trust, he might never have participated in a classroom again. Fortunately, I was able to continue to work with Mike every day until he left the facility.

For some teens, the dollar value of knowledge can be a persuasive selling point that might motivate them to stay in school. We all know that high school graduates earn dramatically more than those who drop out. Kids need to hear it again and again. Legitimate jobs provide money that lasts; slinging drugs can generate big bucks initially, but those dollars will be taken away, one way or another, and jail time doesn't pay well.

Just staying in school isn't enough.

> Honestly, my mentality was about surviving. It was about looking good and acting tougher than the other guy. I really didn't see any sense to school and now it shows. When I came here I did not know
> > there are continents
> > states are different than countries
> > water covers much of the globe
> > I didn't even know why we wouldn't fall off the earth if we were at the bottom
> > I didn't know I was ignorant. I didn't care about knowing anything.
> > > Now I care.
> > > Now I am learning.
> > > Now I can be somebody.
> > > Now I can have worth.
> > > Now I can help make the world a better place,
> > > > some way,
> > > > some day,
> > > > somehow.
> > > Thank you.
> > > (seventeen-year-old boy)

Teens need to learn; they need to be able to present themselves as knowledgeable people who can bring something to the table of life. Ignorance doesn't pay either—personally or professionally. I want the kids to understand the importance of going into the world armed with knowledge and with certification of that knowledge. I try to use humor to help make my point.

Can you imagine these comments being made after interviews or in the work place? The students don't miss how ludicrous it sounds when I say, "I never met someone as stupid as that guy. Let's give him the job," or "That girl doesn't know anything. Let's give her a raise."

No one wants to put himself in embarrassing situations. I like to help kids see how education might change the path of their lives, where they live, and how they live. Students need to think ahead in order to be able to answer questions that may come up in an interview. Why would someone hire me? What do I bring to the job? How can I prepare to be a worthwhile employee? How can I present that worth in an interview? What classes should I take or certifications should I acquire, as a teenager, to have a better chance of both getting and keeping a job?

An uneducated person can count on being the last hired and the first fired. Kids do care about jobs and money. If establishing the connection between knowledge and dollars gets *those* kids wanting to learn, let's use it.

Ask kids to consider applying Bill Gates's famous statement to their lives. He said, "Be nice to nerds. Chances are you'll end up working for one." I imagine many people who went to school with Bill Gates now wish they had been his friend. The friends we choose have values, good and bad, that will rub off on us. What is cool in high school might not be so cool when a person is thirty, trying to get a job to pay the bills.

The compelling book, *The Pact* by Drs. Davis, Jenkins, and Hunt, illustrates the positive results of friendship between three teenage males who were flirting with delinquency but now are doctors and authors of best-selling books. These three young men held each other accountable, using multiple techniques to keep each other in school and studying to make good grades. Our students, likewise, need to find friends who will prod one another to get an education so they can live well in the future.

The lack of knowledge among some youth today is tragic. Ignorance itself is a huge barrier for kids who have fallen so far behind in all aspects of their education that they are too embarrassed to try. Long before job interviews, some students risk shame every day in school or their communities due to lack of knowledge. If we agree that knowledge is power, surely the following quotes from kids in American classrooms illustrate the tragedy, ignorance, and powerlessness these kids will experience if they don't learn and if we don't find a way to reach them.

- "Islands float on water."
- "A silo isn't something on a farm. It's where you put crazy people."
- Looking at a large wall map, a student asked, "What's on the other side of the world?"
- In the book, *Three Cups of Tea*, a poor Pakistani person paid for something in *rupees*. A student said, "Miss, these people are supposed to be poor but he paid in *rubies*. That guy's not poor. He's got bank."
- "The 4th of July is really big in Africa!"
- "How could Confucius have said that in BC? No one was alive BC."
- "Oh, you're just bs-ing me. China can't have more people than Mexico."
- "Pearl Harbor was when they bombed Chinatown in Cali."
- "Shakespeare wrote some of the verses in the Bible."
- "Hitler invaded Cuba."

- "Is Michelangelo Maya Angelou's brother?"
- "The real reason the United States entered World War II is that 'they' tried to steal our oil."
- Seeing the famous picture of George Washington crossing the Delaware, a student said, "That's when the Mexicans took over America."
- "Aliens built the pyramids."

The knowledge vacuum in our schools is unacceptable. Students are falling through the cracks of society, and teachers are burning out. Rather than leading in the world of education, America is slipping, putting the entire future of our nation at risk.

Let's take innovative steps to empower *those* kids to transcend their current journeys and acquire the knowledge that will give them a future. Let's defy the stereotypes of irrelevant classrooms. Let's energize our students, get them on the edge of their seats wondering what they get to learn next. Let's make teaching once again a powerful profession filled with significance and success. To do this, we must free teachers to develop relationships with these students who are hungry for mentors and for relevant curriculum.

When My Priorities Changed, My Behaviors Followed

One day while I was shopping, a young woman came up, introduced herself, and asked if I remembered her. She had been a student in my classes in the detention center. Now, she's a college student with a good job, working her way through school. I asked how she had turned her life around. Her interesting answer was, "I didn't make it the first time I was locked up; I came back four more times. The first times I only wanted to get out, get high, and have fun. But, the fifth time I was there, I realized what I wanted to do with my life. I knew I wanted to work with kids in criminal justice because I've been there; it's what I know. I can help kids."

Then she made this great observation, "When my priorities changed, my behaviors followed."

This quote, painted on the wall, reaches so many kids. They relate to it. It gives them hope and suggests a path to success. The question for students is: What are my priorities? Frankly, many of the teens I work with know neither the meaning of the word *priorities* nor the importance of planning for the future. These kids live moment to moment, day to day. Working toward a goal is often a new and astonishing revelation.

Many young people from dysfunctional homes grow up without mentoring, without any caring adult who listens to them, who is available for advice and ideas, who helps them figure out what they want to do and how to do it. So many kids grow up certain they'll become famous rappers or play for the NBA or NFL. A mentor could certainly help them develop an alternative plan, just in case.

How can a student who is essentially raising himself have a very broad range of options and priorities? How can a young person realize the impact the priorities he chooses will have on his life? Aren't most kids guided and influenced by the behaviors they see around them? If those influences are not positive or have no relevance to his life, he is likely to have priorities that deal with nothing more than survival.

Young people whose lives are limited by difficult home situations and negative influences may not know what the possibilities are for their futures. Indeed, if they have not spent much time in school, haven't read or had significant contact with a variety of ideas and options, or had anyone in their lives who would help them discover alternative options, they may not know how to look beyond the choices that have landed them in a juvenile detention facility.

An important role of a teacher is to become a life coach-mentor for students. Of course it is time consuming, but if we can help a teenager unlock his potential and his aspirations, haven't we made a significant impact in the child's life and in our own? Teachers get the priceless opportunity, along with teaching curriculum, to be perhaps the singular adult to help reclaim a life. When you think back to the best teacher you ever had, that person was very likely someone you have always considered a mentor and role model.

What does a mentor look like to a kid? It is certainly not someone who stands in front of a class and talks or delivers worksheets and assignment deadlines. A mentor is someone who takes the time to listen, to give advice based on facts relevant to the student's life, guides students in learning how to make better choices, and counsels students who are struggling with issues that interfere with their ability to function in the classroom.

Life Is Choices

When a student believes that life is choices, he has a greater probability of achieving success. On the other hand, if he thinks that life happens to him, he is less likely to plan, to work hard, or to accept accountability for his actions.

A young person growing up without positive mentors often flounders and doesn't recognize his ability to determine his life's path in any significant way. He becomes easy prey for gangs and other strong influences that will make decisions for him. A teacher who helps a student realize both the power and the consequences of his choices is giving him a life-altering gift.

> Life is Choices: I know that I've made my fair share of mistakes in my life or I wouldn't be writing this right now right here. You have to make right choices for yourself. Not just for your family. 'Cause it's easy to say, "I'll stay home." But then you run. Choices...As a matter of fact I have no choice in it anymore. Thanks to the choices I've made in my life. All I know at this point I can't keep putting myself and my future at risk. I turn 18 this May and to be honest I so scared 'cause then I don't come back to detention. I go to jail. I truly deeply want to get better to heal myself and not look down upon myself as I always have.
> (seventeen-year-old boy)

One simple tool that a student can use is a diagram of a ladder. He can insert his potential life choices on the rungs as he plans how to attain a goal. A student places his current situation on the bottom rung and a life goal on the top. On each rung, the student places the steps he must take to achieve his goal. He can add as many rungs as he thinks he needs to get from the present to success.

It's important for a student to think and plan what he wants to be or do as an adult, and perhaps doing a ladder for several life options makes more sense than just one. Students with personal goals and ambitions are less vulnerable to outside influences because they have firmly fixed in their minds a path to follow toward a well-thought-out goal. If they are encouraged to talk about what they want to do after high school and how they intend to accomplish it, they are more likely to take the steps necessary to see it through.

It is unlikely that a student, or any of us, will accomplish the climb from the bottom to the top of the ladder with no detours. In reality, most of us may go up a few rungs, come back down when we've made some unfortunate choices, and begin back

---

The Power Pyramid
If I am a girl in a detention center, if I am girl who has dropped out of school, I am at the bottom of the power pyramid. How can I move up on this pyramid of power? I must realize that life is choices. I can make choices that will move me up on that pyramid.

I can get an education.
I can care about others in addition to myself.
I can make a difference in this world.
I can choose behaviors that will help me succeed.
I can choose friends who will help me succeed.
I can help others who have less than I.

Even if now I am at the bottom of the power pyramid, I can find a path that will lead me upward. I will find that path.
(seventeen-year-old girl)

up again. Assuming the person on that ladder has learned from his errors and has taken responsibility for his missteps, he will be able to climb the ladder again, but this time with a greater probability of success and some hard-won knowledge under his belt.

Another way to help teens see the impact of the choices they make is to have them think of their life up to now as a video, a virtual video, and they are the directors. Direct them to push pause when they reach the present and examine their current circumstances. What choices could they make for their futures? When they choose one, they may press play and watch their virtual life play out before them. How did that choice work out? If the result isn't so good, they may hit replay and try another choice.

These are exercises students can do again and again. Ladders and virtual videos of life choices illustrate clearly the importance of their choices. These exercises are powerful, beneficial tools. They are valuable gifts to students who may be experiencing life without much guidance from responsible adults.

After being in my classroom for several weeks during which we came back often to the topic of the importance of choices in constructing a future that is likely to have more positive than negative outcomes, Dahlia wrote the following:

> I finally get it. I've always let others make my choices for me and that isn't going so good. I don't have to just go along. I can actually choose. I have to make choices for myself, not just for my family and my friends. Their lives aren't going so great either. What I know at this point is that I can't keep putting myself and my future at risk anymore. If I keep letting my friends make choices for me, soon I'll have no choices left to make. I know where this will lead me and I don't want jail to be at the top of my ladder. I want to get better to heal myself. And not look down upon myself as I always have. Now at the top of my ladder is living clean. I'm starting to fill it in from the bottom up.

A child in a detention facility has made choices that led him there. A student on the honor roll heading to college has made choices that led there as well. Every child has the right to expect that he will learn in school about choices and what a difference those choices can and will make in his future. No matter what his home or community circumstances, he is not destined to fail if he has the desire to plan for success. He needs just one person to believe with him in the choices that can take him to a better future.

Failure Is for Learning

Failure is a natural and important part of life. It's how we learn to walk, speak, and ride a bike. Nevertheless, failure is scary for kids. Will they be laughed at, will they get in trouble, will a failing grade be exposed in class, will they be ridiculed if they read aloud poorly or answer a question incorrectly, and will a failure ruin their lives? Somehow we've got to convince kids that failure, though painful, is essential to learning. Everybody fails.

Often I congratulate a student when he fails. Perhaps he pointed to India on a map, mistakenly naming it Indonesia. I congratulate him on remembering the beginning of the name of the country; I note that both countries are on the continent of Asia. I praise him for his effort. He is learning and creating an opportunity for learning for the entire class. He is showing leadership by stepping up and volunteering this way. He had the courage to try. He encourages others to feel brave enough to try. It's terrific. He will learn something. Capitalizing on failures, no matter how they occur or how serious they might be, often becomes the great moments for learning. Kids feel victory when they take a chance and answer a question, even if they get it wrong, if I spotlight the moment and congratulate them for having the guts to try.

These moments have more impact if the students have seen me admit my mistakes along the way, saying, "Wow, I really learned something just now, didn't I?" I often point out mistakes I make when I am teaching or outside of school.

When I was in high school, I was an average student in French. Then I missed a week of school for a tour with the youth symphony. I returned on a Saturday, and a friend loaned me a copy of a test they had taken while I was gone. Her intent was honorable as was my studying it before returning to French class on Monday. However, my honor vanished when I was given a make-up test, and it was the same one I had studied. I didn't tell. The next day, my teacher, Madame Leiper, called me aside and, showing me the A+ grade, said, "Marie, I'm sorry to say that I think you have cheated." I adored this teacher and couldn't imagine confessing, so I lied. I swore I had just studied really hard during the week I was gone. I walked out of her room feeling overwhelming shame, but also a profound determination to become an A student of whom she would be proud. I knew I couldn't make all A+s, but I resolved to never score lower than an A. That is the moment I learned how to study. Previously, I had fit studying in around other activities, looking over the notes and pages that had been assigned, but I put little effort into my school work.

After my cheating incident, I found out that studying involved learning everything I could find about the subject: investigating the materials, going beyond the assignment to expand my knowledge, and working as late into the night as all this required. What I had done on the French test was grossly wrong; what I learned from it was life changing. In the spring of that year, this teacher hosted an annual dinner. The highlight of the evening was the awarding of the *Prix d'Honneur*, the prize of honor. She called my name, handed me a certificate, and said privately, "Marie, I want you to know that I understand."

This is an important type of experience to share with kids. Perhaps they, like me, had participated in shameful activities, but one thing a teacher can do is help our kids walk from darkness into light, from dishonor into hope. They are more likely to take our hands along that journey if they believe we have no intention of judging them along the way. Kids need to know that adults have failed. They need to hear us admit it when we mess up, and they need to hear us apologize when it is appropriate. Failure can be a good thing when we learn from it. We need not fear failure; we can improve because of it. When the *r* word, *respect*, is the standard of a classroom, it becomes safe for any of us to fail because failures are treated with respect and even appreciation. Young people learn to empathize and show support for effort and participation. Perhaps most important, all kids feel safer when they know that failure is part of the learning process and not a moment of humiliation. A safe classroom is a place where learning, and failure, can occur safely.

It is possible to get kids to respect the failures of others as well as learning from their own. Frankly, I think they love this novel situation where mistakes are seen as occasions for learning and are accepted as part of being human beings, easing some of their own fears of being mocked publicly.

Kids begin to accept this mutual respect as a norm, and the more it is practiced, the easier it becomes. The goal is to leave each student's dignity intact. The only times I have had this become difficult is when there is a racially motivated desire to put someone down. This is dangerous, and I will not allow that interaction to become the topic or to let it destroy our class and our discussion. When it happens—and it will—I try to find something outside of what they have said to broaden the conflict into a discussion. Using a nonconfrontational and even slightly humorous tone of voice, I might respond as in the following example. Student A says to student B, "Yeah, you think you're so smart coming from your fancy-ass hood, but you'd better not act like you can teach the class." This could become a shouting match and could escalate into something worse. I might say to student B, "Yeah, James, I'm just the teacher and don't get paid much so give me a break." I might say to the accuser, "Justus, in fact you were saying something I liked when you said, 'The next war may be fought over water.' Tell us more." Saying, "You're all just like my sons. Who else can raise your hand and tell me something about how it's often the women and girls who have to walk miles to get water for their families?" to both students or to the class at large will shift the focus and diffuse the tension. It won't be textbook, but it doesn't need to be. Help kids step aside instead of spiraling downward into a continuing and worsening argument. It may take hours of modeling respectful behaviors to reap positive behavior changes, but the tiny steps toward building confidence, healing hurts, and recovering from feelings of failure are essential if learning is to occur.

Before children ever walk into a classroom, they have begun to experience an air-brushed world. They see the beautiful people all around them on television and billboards, in movies and in magazines. It's difficult for teens to believe that they're okay if they're overweight, have zits, don't have a six-pack, or are flat chested. Today people look, or are trying to look, better than anything the world has seen before. Plastic surgery and makeup for children, impossibly thin Barbie dolls and moms, amazing cars, homes, and TVs people can't afford together make a world that is more fantasy than real. Of course this isn't good for kids. My first task as teacher is to help real kids believe they're good enough just as they are and that they are not already losers.

Failures are scarier than they've ever been; to be fat or to screw up used to be bad enough, but today kids see these things posted on Facebook or other social media for their peers and the world at large to see in an instant. Losers are not cool, so it's better not to try than to experience the ravages of failure. Often overanxious parents buy into this can't-fail mentality and do their child's homework. They may cover up unhealthy behaviors such as bullying, cheating, underage drinking, or smoking weed rather than letting their child experience the consequences of his actions.

Young people need to hear Winston Churchill's words: "Success is not final, failure is not fatal: it is the courage to continue that counts."

Iron is forged in fire, diamonds are made by heat and pressure, and pearls are formed when the oyster shell is invaded by an irritant. These are symbols of strength and beauty that are attained by pain, stress, or discomfort. The beauty and power of success come from hard work, and the hardest time to persevere is when we have experienced a failure. But the sweetest triumph is in overcoming a failure by refusing to let it keep us down.

It Is Impossible for a Man to Learn What He Thinks He Already Knows.

—Epictetus

I have noticed a disturbing trend. Frequently, the lower a student's academic performance, the more convinced he is of what he thinks he already knows. Considering the misinformation that abounds on the Internet and elsewhere, this is troubling, especially for those kids who may receive little informed guidance at home.

Often entrenched beliefs involve conspiracy theories, perhaps a strong belief in the Illuminati, a secret organization believed to be made up of the most powerful and influential elite in the world. Conspiracies seem to excuse a young person's behavior. Some kids believe the world is controlled and manipulated by evil, rich, and unscrupulous people, so what chance would a teenager have against such villainous dominance?

Some beliefs I frequently face include the following:

- Bill Gates, Oprah Winfrey, Queen Elizabeth II, and President Barack Obama have built a secret city under Denver International Airport. It's where rich people can go to hide when the Chinese attack us.

- Rappers know what's going on. The proof is that Lil Wayne wrote, "I know what they don't want to tell you."
- President John Kennedy was killed by our government because he was all about peace. He was printing money to help us, and that's when the government decided they had to take him out.
- President Obama is a puppet of Bill Gates, who wants us to go into space and bomb the world.
- Humans have only gone into space seven times, but have never landed on the moon. The government lied to us.
- Swine flu was made by the US government to see how smart people are and to make money (people paying for injections). The same is true of AIDS.
- The government is chipping people at birth to track where they go.
- The government will kill you if you have herpes.
- The US government has cures for cancer, but won't tell because they want the money.
- The government, President George W. Bush in particular, caused 9/11. The planes that hit the twin towers were armed with bombs made by the US government, and the bombs are what really made the buildings go down. The Pentagon was never really hit.

All of these conspiracy theories have had fairly wide support among students, primarily those kids who are making poor grades, and possibly disrupting or ditching classes. Their belief in ideas such as these is strong, and they are often resistant to investigating other suggestions or possibilities.

It may seem strange to go on so long about these theories that are held by many youth in America today. However, preparing for this onslaught of conspiracy theories and misinformation has helped me have materials ready so that a student might readdress what he thinks he already knows. Whenever I start a new topic in class, I do fact checks about key historical figures or subject matter I want the students to learn and familiarize myself with the most popular myths circulating about the topic. For example, when we study Hitler, I am astonished by the "facts" students are convinced are true: he was gay, he was Jewish, he escaped Germany before the end of the war, etc. The list is endless.

In my classroom, I have a number of controversial books, including Hitler's *Mein Kampf*, which I am happy to share, but I also gather lists of journal articles, websites, and other books, so I will be armed with sources that refute the misinformation. When these "facts" come up in class, I pass on these materials to students to study so that they learn to consider possibilities other than the ones they previously believed to be true. Doing this not only corrects gross misunderstandings, but teaches the children through example how to sift through media and how to look for information in a variety of places besides what is immediately at hand for them.

One day, a female student came in telling me all about FEMA internment camps that were detaining thousands of US citizens, who supposedly had found out certain things the government was doing in secret. Fortunately, I had heard this one before, so I was able to give her a pretty interesting article to read that debunked the theory. When she came to class the next day, I asked her if she had read it and what she thought. She lowered her face and said, "I feel like a dumb ass."

Most students aren't easily convinced that alternate possibilities exist with exposure to just one other source. Many students are used to anything and everything on the Internet being their only source of "facts" about life outside the hood, and they have never been taught to distinguish sound sources from utter nonsense. To help students rectify these distorted and firmly held beliefs, it can be helpful to talk about an example such as the famous Tank Man photo taken during the Tiananmen Square

Massacre in 1989. If I explain that information about this event has never been available inside China because of vigilant government censorship, it helps kids realize that simply googling something may not always be reliable, and that accuracy and inaccuracy can exist side by side.

On the twenty-fifth anniversary of this tragedy, the few people in China who knew of the event wanted to evade censors and display the famous picture. Because this was not possible, they actually substituted big yellow rubber ducks for the tanks and were able to briefly post this clever substitution online before Chinese censors realized what was happening and quickly blocked it, blocking even the words *big, rubber,* and *duck*. I am proud to remind students that in the United States we do have freedom of speech and freedom of the press—a luxury not granted in many parts of the world. Nonetheless, something posted on a computer represents our constitutional freedoms; it does not guarantee accuracy.

Most kids walk into my classroom with fiercely held beliefs in urban myths and conspiracy theories. They have never been taught the skills to discern truth from rumor; fear and necessity train them to accept that what the gang believes must be universally true. Slowly and steadily discovering a larger world by encountering a variety of authoritative sources of information about the true facts behind this rampant misinformation can be powerful and freeing for students. It is especially so for those who have allowed themselves to follow others who appeared more powerful and knowledgeable than they. Just as a dictator has difficulty ruling educated people, gang or youth culture thrives where there is a vacuum of learning. Indoctrination must not be allowed to triumph over enlightenment, and an alive, vibrant classroom is where groupthink ends and personal authenticity can begin. It is ironic that, for many of my students, the first time they have been free to learn is in a juvenile prison.

Education begins with the exposure to and search for new ideas. My commitment to *those* kids is to help them learn so much that is true and verifiable that when they go back to their neighborhoods, communities, or even the streets, they will be able to act as teachers and encouragers to those who previously have merely followed the leader of the pack.

Success Is Attitude. Attitude Is 10 Percent What Happens to You and 90 Percent How You Respond.

A child may have been dealt a difficult or even hellish hand in the life he was given. Although the realities may be sad, even tragic, the choices with which he responds are crucial. His response will be life altering, life giving, or life ending.

- Helen Keller became blind and deaf before she turned three.
- Oprah Winfrey survived an abusive childhood.
- President Nelson Mandela endured twenty-seven years in prison before becoming president of South Africa.
- Bethany Hamilton, a surfer who lost an arm in a shark attack at the age of fourteen, returned to surfing one month after this appalling event.
- Lopez Lomong, abducted at age six, endured ten years in a refugee camp and became an Olympic athlete, who was chosen to carry the American flag in the Beijing Olympics.
- Nick Vujicec was born with no arms or legs, but is now a successful motivational speaker, encouraging others to lead productive lives.

The stories of people overcoming incredible obstacles are inspiring and are illustrations of this quote. I am often moved by my students' stories. I listen, I care, and I want to support them as they consider their choices and move forward with their lives. At some point, their response must carry them past their tragedy and into a positive life attitude that embraces possibility and perseverance. Students who are trying to survive chaos and uncertainty are deeply affected and inspired by the stories of those who have overcome adversity.

Quentin's story was one of the most incredible and inspiring in all my years teaching kids who had so much stacked against them. Quentin was easy to like and easy to want to protect. He smiled, he tried hard, and he got along pretty well with other kids, but he was painfully and unnaturally short. One day, Quentin told me this story. His dad, whom he had never met, got out of prison and came home. Quentin was about nine. His mom was scared and held tightly to a younger sibling as Quentin, who had long tried to be man of the house, stood between his dad and his mom and the young child. What followed is inexplicable.

As Quentin tried to calm the situation and to get acquainted, he noticed his dad looking all over the house—even in the garage. His dad began yelling at them as the mom and younger child fled to the bedroom and locked the door. Quentin tried to get his dad to leave. He told him they'd try to talk again the next day. Horrifically, when his dad came in from the garage, he had brought some power tools, including an electric drill. By the time he left, Quentin's father had drilled holes into Quentin's knees.

Quentin loved to learn the poems, and he asked me to include one he had written. I explained that even though I would love to use all the poems students had written, I had chosen not to do so as this was a social studies class, not language arts. He accepted my decision, but on his last day in my class he said, "Miss, I know I'm going to make it. I am going to succeed. If someday I can prove to you that I'm succeeding, will you use my poem?" I said that I'd be happy to, even though I had no idea what this really meant. A couple of years later, I was told that I had a visitor in the lobby, and there was Quentin waiting for me. With a huge smile on his face, he handed me an envelope that contained an invitation to his high school graduation and, in another envelope, a copy of his letter of acceptance to a state university. He said, "Now, Ms. Sklar, will you use my poem?" Needless to say, I did.

Lou Holtz, football coach at the University of South Carolina, once said, "Show me someone who has done something worthwhile, and I'll show you someone who has overcome adversity." If our kids—*those* kids—find ways to turn their life tragedies into triumphs, they will be on the path to success both in school and in life.

The Only Thing Necessary for the Triumph of Evil Is for Good Men to Do Nothing.
—Edmund Burke

When the norms of decent society break down as, for example, they did during the Holocaust, what codes of conduct does one follow? In such times of horror, how does man live above animalistic instincts to kill or be killed? Can personal moral authority prevail when ethical codes of justice in society as a whole are no longer honored?

The students who sit in my classroom are living in this broken slice of society. They learn to kill or be killed. Decent society for them is waking up alive the next morning. Codes of justice are those dictates passed down by the strongest gang in the hood. It is no surprise that these kids have never considered that they can play a part in making changes to help break the cycle of societal breakdown or that they have a choice about what to do with their own lives and that they can become more than drug dealers and thugs. One of the best ways to get the attention of these kids is to find examples of human beings who did something to resist the triumph of evil and bring them into the classroom for discussion.

True heroes are not hard to find, and they grab the attention and imagination of those kids whose lives have not been touched by heroic figures. Irena Sender worked as a nurse in the Warsaw Ghetto during the occupation by Nazis. She courageously rescued more than twenty-five hundred Jewish infants and children by hiding them in a burlap bag or a toolbox. Any sounds the children made were covered by the sound of her dog that she had trained to bark when she was questioned by Nazis. Six staff members died protecting the lives of their students at Sandy Hook Elementary School in Newtown, Connecticut. A teacher died at Columbine High School in Littleton, Colorado, and many other teachers have been killed or seriously injured at schools where tragic violence took place. Most of these teachers were either

> I want to be a hero because I want to do and fight for something I believe in and help people who believe in the same thing I do. I want to be a hero to my kids when I have some and help them believe in what I believe and show them that they could help the world in their own way.
> (sixteen-year-old boy)

shielding children or trying to reason with a shooter. Some moviegoers at the Aurora, Colorado, theater massacre lost their own lives while protecting others. Firefighters and first responders regularly put their lives in jeopardy for the well-being of others. These are all stories that capture the attention of students and spark discussion.

With the prevalence of online posting, we are inundated with videos of barbarous fights, horrific bullying, gang initiations, or inappropriate sexual behavior. Occasionally, we see YouTube examples of kids who have intervened to stop a fight or prevent others from participating in violence or sexual abuse. Sadly, we are more frequently exposed to the reality that people usually avoid interference, even when they know it is the right thing to do.

Teaching kids in school about the Nelson Mandelas of the world will change their definition of what is possible and their own perceptions of what they can do in their own little corner of the world.

Students who have studied the Holocaust and have internalized the significance of what man did to man are more likely to have the courage to stand up for another kid or to protect another kid from violence and intimidation. Students who have studied the champions of nonviolence and appreciate the undaunted courage of Gandhi, Mandela, and Martin Luther King Jr. can and will make choices that are decent and brave, making their lives and our world a better place. Students who have read an inspirational book or who have encountered the possibility and the importance of an education can change our schools and our communities. Students who know more than the survival of the fittest, the toughest, and the loudest are the kids who are better equipped to succeed.

Once students have encountered true heroism on a grand scale, they can and will translate the lessons into their everyday reality. They will have the courage to stop a fight on school grounds or in the neighborhood. They will have the courage to shut down cell phones to prevent others from taking pictures that might otherwise be posted online to humiliate one student or glorify another for thug-like behavior. They will have the guts to sit beside a nerd in the lunchroom, putting aside concerns of what their friends might think. They will have the courage to go to school when all their friends are ditching. They will find the pluck, the marvelous audacity, to say no to gangs, drugs, and alcohol.

In the everyday experience of these teens, evil often triumphs, but when individuals who have displayed courage are put before the students, they are inspired to attempt leadership that is positive and for which they might afterward feel pride. We must reach *those* kids; *those* kids are unaccustomed to feeling proud of themselves. What a moment it would be if they could feel proud and reduce the evil in the world at the same time.

10 Poem Day

Friday is Poem Day—a tradition that has become a centerpiece for kids who are trying to find ways to express their feelings about the harshness and confusion of their lives. This day also provides an opportunity for kids who want to do and learn more and for those who want to try something different. An innovative teacher can

> **After reading "The Rose That Grew from Concrete" by Tupac Shakur:**
>
> Nobody including themselves think they can do any better than they ever have before. But just because the teacher starts to believe in them they actually start to "rise beyond and succeed." I've grown up the same way. I never got support from either of my parents but now that I'm old enough to support myself I can turn my life around so I feel like I am the same rose. And to be honest with you I don't think I would be ready to support myself if it wasn't for your class and memorizing "The Rose That Grew from Concrete." Miss, you are the reason that I won't come back [to the detention center]. (I mean that in a good way.)
>
> (sixteen-year-old boy)

develop his own variation of poem day to adapt and stretch the basic curriculum. The poem program in our social studies class functions this way.

Each new student is given a sheet with the basic poem set. It consists of "Self Talk," which I wrote, and four Tupac Shakur poems: "The Rose that Grew from Concrete," "Where there's a will there's a way," "God," and "If in my quest 2 achieve my goals." The student can take the sheet with him and memorize any poems that interest him. We do not use class time for memorization. It is the student's choice and responsibility to do the work on his own time. On Fridays, students can share what they've learned. The first time a student recites "Self Talk" (see p. 2), he receives a Snickers bar and may contribute one hundred pennies, which I provide, to whatever charity we are supporting that year. At any point during the following weeks, he may again recite "Self Talk" on Poem Day, but will receive only one Jolly Rancher as a reward. Each of the Tupac poems is worth one Jolly Rancher—a lesser prize as those poems are shorter and easier to memorize because they rhyme.

After memorizing "Self Talk," a student may choose from among the huge selection of poems I provide to study and memorize for the following Friday. Theoretically, he can earn a Snickers bar every week.

I mentioned that a student who memorizes one of the Snickers poems can donate one hundred pennies to the charity we support in any given year. We alternate between a local charity, usually one that supports children and education, and an international organization that has a similar mission statement. I want the students to know not only about the suffering in the world, but also to be able to make a positive difference. The reason for this monetary contribution is to empower kids to effect change in a concrete way. I want them to know that while they are improving their own lives by the choices they are learning to make, they can also help others less fortunate than themselves. I supply the rolls of pennies, but they do the memorization work to make a difference in lives around the world. In this way, students can become humanitarians and heroes. We use the symbol H^2, heroes squared.

After a student successfully recites one of the Snickers poems, he comes to the front of the classroom to drop rolls of pennies into a donation bucket. Other students congratulate him, often accompanied by applause. The most common statement I hear from students as they drop their pennies into the bucket is

"Oh Miss, I wish my mother could see me. She'd be so proud." Apathy, not common in room 101, is totally absent on Friday.

Each time a student memorizes one of these poems, his name goes on the list of humanitarians on the classroom door. The list grows longer as the year progresses; almost always, it covers the door from top to bottom by June. The kids do check to make sure their names are there. It is yet another method to show the success that is possible to all who enter.

I have a file on a table by my desk that is filled with a large selection of poems from which the kids may choose. The following list is a selection of ones the kids often choose to memorize:

- "Invictus"   William Ernest Henley
- "America the Beautiful"   Katharine Lee Bates
- "If"   Rudyard Kipling
- "The Dash"   Linda Ellis
- "Don't Quit"   Author Unknown
- "O Captain! My Captain"   Walt Whitman
- "No Man Is an Island"   John Donne
- "Wasted Time"   Dave LeFave
- "Star Spangled Banner"   Francis Scott Key
- "Self Talk"   Mary Duerksen Sklar
- "Deepest Fear"   President Nelson Mandela
- "Alone"   Maya Angelou
- "Caged Bird Sings"   Maya Angelou
- "Phenomenal Woman"   Maya Angelou
- "Still I Rise"   Maya Angelou
- "If I Knew" (9/11)   Author Unknown
- "The Road Not Taken"   Robert Frost
- "Stopping by the Woods"   Robert Frost
- "The New Colossus"   Emma Lazar

There is another file of even more difficult writings; these are not for the faint of heart. The reward is slightly higher, allowing the students to donate more rolls of pennies. Below is a partial list of the more difficult works.

- The Bill of Rights
- The Gettysburg Address—President Abraham Lincoln
- "I Have a Dream" speech (first half)—Reverend Martin Luther King Jr.
- "I Have a Dream" speech (second half)—Reverend Martin Luther King Jr.
- "Runaway Train"—Geoffrey Canada
- "My Name Is Meth"—variously attributed
- Declaration of Independence (portion beginning with "When in the Course of human events…" and ending with "…to alter their former Systems of Government.")—President Thomas Jefferson

Poem Day has come to serve a variety of purposes. My original intent was to introduce *those* students to poetry. It was my belief that most of them probably had never read poetry and would be surprised to find that they might relate to the thoughts and feelings expressed by some of these writers. To my delight, the reading and memorization of poetry, even some of the more difficult material, has become one of the most talked-about and interesting weekly projects in my classroom. It is particularly heartening to see teenage boys throw themselves into such an activity and participate enthusiastically in the discussion of the ideas addressed in the poems. Earning the right to contribute to charitable organizations is an added bonus. Most students never imagined they would be able to do this and are able to grow in confidence and respect for themselves.

11 Change of Pace

Routine procedures, norms, and expectations will enhance security; this is especially important for kids who come from lives marked by chaos. Having said that, I think that periodically a teacher may want to change the pace to ensure that what is familiar doesn't become stifling or too predictable to be interesting. The following are ideas I have used to energize a class that needs a boost or a new program to involve kids on a different level.

Early Morning Coffee Club

I love inviting a small group of the students to join me an hour before school for coffee club. They can come once and check it out with no future commitment. Some students think it is a very confusing invitation and expect it to be boring: "You mean we're just going to sit there and talk? What about? Why?" The group must be small in number—five at most—otherwise the discussions may lack intimacy, trust, and impact.

The first time I tried it, four of the five invitees showed up. Some knew each other, some did not. Everyone seemed nervous. We all introduced ourselves and shared something about our lives. Sitting in the circle with the kids, I became both facilitator and a group member. They were quite insistent that we should have a specific topic, but nobody wanted to suggest one.

I work for an excellent school district that has as its motto "To inspire every student to think, to learn, to achieve, to care." I asked the members of our first-ever coffee club which of those values they thought was most important, and the conversation took off. Some believed learning was most important. After all, knowledge is power. But another young man said he believed that knowledge is worthless without caring. Another stated that learning is worthless without action and without achieving something. Another pointed out that thinking was the basis of everything we do, and on it went. They were astonished when I said we needed to wrap it up. The hour had flown by, and discussion about the district motto was still continuing passionately.

They were all back the next week, and the fifth student also came as he had gotten the word that it was a cool thing to do. They wanted to meet more often; other kids begged to join or wanted me to start a second group, etc. They agreed on a maximum number for each group in order to maintain the intimacy and trust of the group discussions. Relationships flourished in these mornings, education became relevant, and *those* kids began making more positive choices while disrupting class less.

This activity highlights nearly all of the values I try to bring to the classroom. The students feel their opinions are valued and that they would not have been included in the group unless I had respect for what they as individuals could bring to it. They also listen to each other and learn about the others' lives and experiences; thus, they are building relationships that serve to smooth the waters when there might otherwise be conflict in the classroom. The more *those* kids become invested in each other and in the class, the less likely they are to resort to behaviors that distract from the important educational work we are doing.

These coffee clubs also help the students to see the relevance of classroom topics in their own lives. There is an endless list of topics: perhaps something from the school fight song or the state motto. The motto for Kansas, translated, is To the Stars through Difficulties. Choosing a quote of a famous entertainer will get their attention and enforce the concept of relevance. For example, using this statement by Jay Z, which is most likely familiar to young students, can let them discuss the hurts and disappointments they've experienced and can segue into lessons being taught in the classroom: "When you're growing up, your dad is your superhero. Once you've let yourself fall that in love with someone, once you put him on such a high pedestal and he lets you down, you never want to experience that pain again."

Whatever topic we might discuss on a given day can tie into something we have studied in class. Even just drinking a cup of coffee can bring up fair trade of coffee beans or environmental impact related to disposable cups.

Soup

There will be days when a class isn't going great or when we need to do something unexpected to grab the kids' interest and to energize them and increase their participation in a different way. One option is making virtual soup.

I keep a huge soup pot and a large wooden spoon in a cabinet in my classroom. When I pull them out, I ask students to tell me ingredients they would choose to prepare a spicy, really hot soup. They add the imaginary ingredients, and I stir. Hot, piquant soup tastes the way it does because of the ingredients the students choose to add such as chiles, tomatoes, jalapeños, cumin, and garlic. We prepare and then taste delicious imaginary bites of our spicy soup. Next, we prepare another, milder soup such as chicken noodle or creamy cheese soup. Again, the students suggest and add the imaginary ingredients; I merely stir and affirm their choices.

We compare the soups, discussing why they are so different from one another. Of course the difference in the taste is because of which ingredients the students have chosen to add. Preparation of virtual soup morphs into the previously mentioned quote: "Life Is Choices." What choices made the soup hot or mild? What choices have brought each of us to the present point in our lives? How does our concern for what others want in the soup affect how we make the soup? The questions and answers go on and on.

The kids are again engaged in the class, its relevance is restored, and usually relationships are formed or strengthened. They take the soup metaphor with them from the classroom and continue to mull over the choices they make.

String of Beads

Another tool I keep in my cabinet is a long string of beads. Each bead represents a choice in my life: bad choices are ugly, clunky beads; shiny, multi-colored, interesting beads represent the good choices. The resulting strand of beads constitutes my whole life.

No life would have all the same beads. We make mistakes—some more harmful than others. We take detours. We take questionable actions, but we also learn and make improvements in our lives over time. All the beads remain. If we learn from the errors of others, we add beads to our strand that will be more beautiful than if we continue to learn everything the hard way by making all the errors ourselves. Regardless, we will continue to add beads as our lives progress.

By showing my string of beads, with all sorts of colors and shapes, I can show these students that a single ugly bead does not mean that the whole string is ruined. Kids can see a visual representation of their choices and realize that they have the power to choose what color or shape the next bead can have. If they don't want any more ugly beads, they can choose wisely or incorporate the lessons learned from history or a classmate to improve the overall appearance of their own strings. A good way to increase the likelihood of adding more attractive, colorful beads is to surround oneself with friends who share similar, positive goals.

Anytime I can use something tactile, I do. This is a tool I can only show the kids in my classroom as they are not allowed to have beads or string in the detention center, but the lesson this string of beads illustrates is effective in helping them think about the impact that the accumulation of choices—good or bad—makes. Sometimes I have the kids draw their own life as a string of beads and have them write a description of what each of the beads represents, or we may have a discussion not only about the beads already on their strings, but about the beads they would like to add.

There are excellent poems that relate to choices that work well with the discussions about the string of beads. Some I've used successfully include "The Dash" by Linda Ellis, "Don't Quit" by Author Unknown, "Wasted Time" by Dave LeFave, "Greatest Fear" by Marianne Williamson, and "Two Roads" by Whitney Welch. By reading published poems about choices, students learn that they are not alone in the struggle to choose wisely, and perhaps they gain the courage to do so after reading what someone else has written.

Heroes in Every Subject

Every curriculum area has its heroes. High-risk students—*those kids*—need heroes to whom they can relate. Often the people close to them have presented more obstacles than inspiration in their lives. Although every child cannot have a live mentor whom he can meet with and talk to, at least he should be able to read about a person to look up to and to emulate.

The heroes do not need to represent any particular subject area as long as the students can relate to the story. Mawi Asgedom, who wrote the books *Of Beetles & Angels* and *The Code*, is a superb hero, and I think every classroom that has copies of his books is richer for it. Mawi was born in Ethiopia. He was seven when he and his family arrived in the United States after spending three years in a refugee camp in Sudan. He grew up in the Chicago suburb of Wheaton; his family survived on very little, but he worked hard in school and made choices that led him to a full-tuition scholarship at Harvard University. He graduated with top honors, receiving a degree in American history and giving the commencement address at his graduation in 1999. Since graduating from Harvard, Mawi has dedicated himself to inspiring teenagers.

Maya Angelou's autobiography, *I Know Why the Caged Bird Sings*, or Jeanette Walls's memoir, *The Glass Castle*, could provide hope and a form of long-distance mentoring by the examples they offer. Maya Angelou's autobiography is a poignant account of a life marked by determination, love, and achievement. The story of her surviving rape, overcoming tragedy, and choosing life with worth and meaning will resonate with young people who are trying to survive their own lives. Jeanette Walls's memoir depicts a child's attempt to rescue herself in a family that steals her childhood. When kids have no option but to take on the parenting in the household, their lives are changed forever. Sadly, this situation is not uncommon in the lives of *those* kids.

No teacher has far to look for heroes. A math teacher can find a hero who overcame difficulties and achieved success in the story of Jaime Escalante. In the film *Stand and Deliver*, we see his incredible story. Jaime Escalante believed in kids—troubled kids, poor kids, angry kids, *those* kids. He resolved to provide high-level math classes in a school where they were not offered as no one thought the students were capable of doing the work. Mr. Escalante absolutely refused to take no for an answer from administrators or kids. When the time for standardized testing came, guess what? They passed! His success rate in motivating and his methods of relating to kids were extraordinary. He was a person many students wanted to emulate, and many teachers and other adults saw him as a mentor whose approach, if followed, worked wonders in the classroom.

What may be even more remarkable about Jaime Escalante is his own story. When he came to America from Bolivia, he was already a teacher, but spoke no English. He worked as a busboy, a cook, and a factory worker; he taught himself English and completed another college degree. He began teaching in Los Angeles at the age of forty-seven.

When Jaime Escalante died in 2010, he was the best-known teacher in the country, and his obituary was prominently displayed in newspapers across the nation, including the *Los Angeles Times* and the *New York Times*. In the *Los Angeles Times*, Edward James Olmos, who played Escalante in *Stand and Deliver*, said, "Jaime didn't just teach math. Like all great teachers, he changed lives."

Troubled kids are in every school district, not just in the movies or in schools connected to juvenile detention centers, and they are all inspired by the lives of real heroes. Learning that there are good people in this world who deserve to be admired and emulated can make a huge difference in the lives of kids who have never dreamed that such people existed.

Unique Vocabulary

Allowing a unique vocabulary might be one component of making a place welcoming to all, including *those* kids who do not expect to fall in love with learning. The kids in my class have been exposed to offensive language since birth and use it almost as easily as breathing. To them, it has lost all of its thunder by its having become so common.

I am offended by swearing and will not allow it in class. To me, swearing is a shoddy way to express oneself, appealing to the ignoble aspects of humanity rather than to a higher level of thought and expression.

Seemingly unrelated, I decided that as a social studies teacher, it would be a disgrace if students left my social studies classes not knowing words such as apartheid, slavery, bigotry, and famine. I wanted these words and their meanings to be keenly understood by each student. How I could convince students to understand and to use important words while eliminating the offensive ones became my dilemma. The solution found its way into our classroom.

One day a student dropped the *f* bomb. I turned to him and looked as dramatically shocked as I could. I told him that if he wanted to use a word to really offend someone, use one that at least showed some awareness. I told him that I knew a word that was way worse than the one he had just used. He looked confused, then asked what I meant. I said, "Try *famine*; it will at least show you have some knowledge and will sure surprise the other guy." To say that the kids were intrigued would be an understatement. They wanted an *a* word. We spent a few days on this one, because the word needed to be a really nasty, stinky word. What could be stinkier than *apartheid*? Since then, we've added *slavery* for the *s* word, and eventually *bigotry* for the *b* word.

> I sit in here, in an 8 x 10 room,
> I often wonder, is this my impending doom?
>
> "Shirts tucked in, pants pulled up."
> I drink my water from a Styrofoam cup
>
> I've done the crime, now I'm doing the time.
> I do not know when I'll be free,
> But to be honest, it doesn't matter to me.
>
> I always say: "I won't be back,"
> But here I am, right back in the sack.
>
> I look out my window, what do I see?
> The things I love, so far away,
> But I'm stuck in here again today.
>
> A PR bond, or 0-2,
> Something old, or something new?
> I know this all is oh so wrong, & that's why I write this
>
> So hopefully you all will see, this life is not for you, & it's not free.
>
> (sixteen-year-old boy)

One time, I thought this idea would surely cost me my job. A superintendent came to visit the class and, of course, a student told him that in this class we are allowed to use the *f* word; another chimed in with the same information about the *a*, the *s*, and the *b* words as well. The superintendent paled visibly, at which time the students began to explain that in room 101 the words meant famine, apartheid, slavery, and bigotry. He asked the students to discuss each of them, which the students were proud and happy to do. Before the superintendent left, he congratulated the students on the knowledge they had acquired. Needless to say, the kids loved it.

This idea is easy to adapt to any subject. A language arts teacher uses this effectively in her classroom. Her *a* word is *adverb*. Another has found it effective in math, where his *f* word is *finite*. It works for some classes, but would be an irresponsible disaster in others. The teacher will be inspired to try it if the situation in her classroom calls for it.

Books

I believe in the power of multicultural reading material that takes a student out of his hood or his known environment. We need to bring the world into our classrooms, and thus I have a lending library for my students. Initially, my friends donated books, and later my school district funded books to be shared from my classroom. I love introducing a student to a book that opens a new part of the world, a new outlook, and new ideas. The lending library in my room is quite different from a traditional library. Students who want a book take one and bring it back when they have finished reading it; there is neither a time limit nor any fines. It's open sharing with absolutely no red tape. Some of the books have been almost worn out with love, not vandalism.

Throughout the school year, I have a list of books that qualify for a certificate stating the student's successful participation in an advanced reading program. When a student tells me he has finished a book from this list, I meet with him to discuss it and ask questions to verify that he has read and understood the book. At that point, I print a certificate that demonstrates his successful participation in our Reading for Excellence program. A student may merely like to have a certificate to keep or, in the case of incarcerated youth, may want to show it to a judge as proof of the good decisions he is making and as an indication of the improved choices he may make in his life.

In addition to having books with fictional stories, trials, and triumphs from around the world, I also keep plenty of autobiographies on hand. Reading someone else's story enlarges one's world regardless of whose story it is, but it also allows students to see that their own stories are unique and that each of them has moments worthy of sharing. Kids are interested in their own lives. Aren't we all?

After students are exposed to a few famous autobiographies, I will assign my students to write their own. I usually try to shift the emphasis about what they should write. Sometimes I ask to include something really good in their lives and something horrendous or maybe to share one memorable event from every five-year chunk of their lives. Perhaps they could write about their goals—what they have been and what they are now. Sometimes I have kids interview each other and present what they learned to the class in the form of an oral biography. With students who are ready for an extra challenge, I have them write or tell their autobiographies from another person's point of view; what would that person say about my student's life?

My experience has shown that using autobiographies or biographies can turn a class that has lost its focus into a class that is succeeding in terms of effectively connecting to the students and their lives outside the classroom. Choosing autobiographies carefully allows us to teach within our specific curriculum areas, while simultaneously engaging the whole child so the lessons are carried beyond the classroom doors and applied in the real world.

Film

I think there is room for film in the classroom, especially clips that make school subjects relevant to the students. This does not mean we sit and watch videos in place of doing schoolwork. However, film can help young people enlarge their world or experience a vital concept in a palpable manner. I frequently use video clips as attention grabbers at the beginning of class. Showing intense scenes from movies or clips of great actors giving famous speeches from classic literature can bring the subjects alive like no lecture can. For example, if I were teaching language arts, I might share hilarious grammar bloopers that are easy to find on YouTube. Math phenomena and amazing moments in science are equally fascinating and can grab kids' interest. These clips can intrigue and challenge kids, preparing the way for what I have to teach. I may also spend the last ten minutes or so of class sharing film clips that dramatically, visually illustrate what we have been studying.

12 Checking In

I believe that periodically taking time to check in with kids saves time and heads off problems. Teenagers have a lot on their minds; from one day to the next, things can change radically in their lives that affect how things will go for them and, thus, for all of us in the classroom. The first days of a school year or semester and the initial days after a vacation especially need to include time for checking in.

The turnover of students where I work is very high; this is also true of many schools today. I make certain that I personally welcome each new student as I would someone who is visiting my home for the first time. I try to put him at ease or, at the very least, let him know I recognize it is difficult to be the new kid in class. When I approach a new student, I might say, "Hi, my name is Mary Sklar. I have two sons, and I love to travel." I will ask questions to try to find an area of common interest. I am a big sports fan, which is a huge help in starting conversations with the students who come into my class. When we are seated in the circle on a day we are checking in, each student shares something about himself. New students are encouraged to participate, but are free to wait until they feel more at home in the group.

> I was afraid to know you
> I was afraid to like you.
> When I liked you
> I was afraid to love you
> But now that I love you,
> I'm afraid to lose you.
>
> (seventeen-year-old girl)

I'll never forget a routine check-in that started with students mentioning that they like to race BMX bikes, their plans to play in the NFL, etc. Then a student who was seventeen years old and had been in class all year said, "My name is Ryan, and my parents got divorced." I said how sorry I was and asked if this had just happened over the break. He responded, "No, it happened when I was two." This young man was in pain, and he needed the release of sharing it. He had a history of ditching school and misbehaving in class. Suddenly, I understood why. On this day, he felt safe enough and the relationships were strong enough that he could share what had been eating away at his heart for years. His turnaround began that day.

Having students share what is going on in their lives around the circle is not the only way to check in with students. Sometimes I set up a class mailbox so that kids can write notes to me privately about anything they want to share. Sometimes it is safety concerns; sometimes ideas for class; and sometimes they write of personal problems they want to tell me about confidentially. I always check the box. The next day, I discreetly hand response notes to each student who writes.

Also, students know they can ask to meet with me during my planning period if they have an urgent need to talk. I need my planning period, but I am willing to share it when necessary. It is not a counseling time. I am not a therapist and am adamant about that. I would call it primarily a time of listening, and that alone can be powerful.

Periodic check-ins give students a chance to talk about what they desperately need to share. Taking time to listen is the first step toward building relationships between teacher and student, without which there can be no connection between what the kids experience in their day-to-day lives and the subject material in the classroom. Kids are more willing to study and learn history, geography, math, and literature if they feel physically safe, know their voices are heard, and when they can respect and are respected by their teacher.

13 Hurt People Hurt People

When I encounter a student who is particularly angry or hostile, either acting out or unusually withdrawn—often one of *those* kids who disrupts class and makes learning difficult for everyone, I know this is probably a child who has been seriously hurt. It might have been caused by abandonment, physical or sexual abuse, or something else that has been deeply harmful. In fact, I am learning that the more difficult the child, the more seriously that child has been hurt. Indeed, hurt people do hurt people. I approach such a child slowly and with care. I don't want to bring gasoline to a fire that is already burning.

Basic practices in room 101 include the simplest of components, all of which are focused on reducing the risk of inadvertently causing harm to a person who is already struggling. These basic rules go a long way toward keeping the classroom from exploding on a day when we may have several kids who are struggling to contain their emotions.

- We honor the *r* word. Respect is king.
- We listen to one another.
- We find something good or positive in what students say.
- We care.
- We show support.

The key to making these basic rules work is to follow them even when correcting students who violate one of them. When a student is disrespectful, for example, instead of giving into the temptation of retorting in kind to their words or putting the student in his place by issuing ultimatums or dishing out severe punishment, I may say, "I do not appreciate or allow anyone to talk to me or to the class in that manner. I value all of you, and I value our class too much to go there." By emphasizing the value each student has, including the disrespectful student, the tone of the class is raised, the kids see respectful responses in action, and the interruption to the class itself is minimized. The basic rules of the class must be followed even if the end result is removal of a student from the classroom. The integrity of the class must be maintained, but no student needs to be shamed in the process. No one wins in a humiliation contest.

I want to make one thing very clear. It is a tragedy that in some facilities the teacher has been denied access to common-sense options to reach students. Perhaps this comes from a misguided understanding of kindness or caring, but chaos results when the policymakers in a school or detention facility confuse logical consequences with being punitive. Detention facilities in particular need to allow and even encourage a program that permits logical consequences to play out, whether they are positive or negative. A detention facility, in a sense, provides the parenting of young people who never had decent parenting in their own homes.

If a student starts a fight, threatens another person, throws an object at another person, or participates in any type of violent behavior, he must be removed from the education setting. I suggest he be gone for a minimum of twenty-five hours, a full school day plus the next class of the teacher in which the act occurred. This is an example of a logical consequence. If a student causes harm, he is not welcome to return immediately.

He must take time, think, write letters of apology, and ask to visit with people involved, so he can apologize. After making amends as best he can, the student may return to class. Our schools and detention facilities must do their part to keep classrooms safe so that education can occur. Not allowing natural consequences punishes everyone. The kids who are trying to attend class and learn deserve a setting that is physically secure.

Teachers who are trying hard to relate and teach kids must know that their facility is safe. And offending students are being ill-treated if we fail to teach them which behaviors are not allowed in society.

✌︎

I have found that many students are desperate to say what is on their minds, and in my class they can do so with no fear of being punished for what they are feeling. I have a stack of challenge-paper topics such as the one Javontae wrote when he joined me for coffee before school. His was titled, "Hurt People Hurt People." His home life was unspeakably horrific, and he had been deeply hurt. He needed a safe place to learn and to heal, and he found that in room 101. We as teachers, not mental health specialists, cannot treat those kids, but we can create spaces where restoration can occur and education can then become meaningful in the student's life.

> **Hurt People**
>
> People that are hurt in their life feel low about themselves. That is the reason why they choose to hurt and abuse others....Every hurt person doesn't just hurt one person. So the number has increased; the number of hurt people has gone way up, and will continue to rise if people do not take a stand to stop the abuse in their lives. It takes one person to start the abuse, but it really only takes one to stop. Let's hold hands with one another and then let's see if the tide indeed can begin to turn.
>
> (fifteen-year-old boy)

Other challenge papers have titles such as "Life Stinks," "What I Wish," "My Life Dreams Are Made of," "What Can I Do When I Can't Take It Anymore?" and "The Changes I Have to Make: The Changes I Will Make." Under the title, I fill the rest of the page, front and back, with lines, which give kids plenty of room to vent, to pour their hearts and stresses onto the paper.

The subtle message I give students by assigning these challenge papers is that someone does care and that someone is listening. I use these challenges for a variety of purposes, but the primary one is communication. I may substitute one for a routine assignment, or I may use it as a starter for a coffee group discussion topic before or during school. These papers and topics are bridges to students, tools to develop a relationship with a student, and a proffered hand that is intended to draw the student into a positive experience with school and with lifelong education.

Many of these hurt young people are about out of steam, out of tolerance for any additional stress. They are more motivated to strike out than we are inclined to be patient. We need to develop practices that do not fuel their fires: practices that instill a sense of relationship, safety, and belonging. As this occurs, inch-by-inch, learning may begin. The more I get to know *those* kids, the more I like teaching them. The more I like teaching them, the more they want to be in class to learn rather than to disrupt and destroy.

I like to infuse each day with many positive reinforcements of respect, caring, listening, and support for every student's contributions, even if the most obvious is simply showing up to class. A simple affirmation is easy to give and may help put out some of the fires of abuse: "I'm glad you were here today," "I hope I'll see you tomorrow," "I appreciate what you said today." Perhaps after hearing such comments, these hurting young people will hurt others less because of the experiences they have had in class.

14 Public Recognition of Success

It's hard to overstate the importance of public recognition of students' success. Many of *those* kids have experienced years of academic failure. If a student is expecting failure, he is apt to find it. His guard will be up so that no teacher, no test will expose his shortcomings. They are accustomed to failing and to public embarrassment—both elements of their dislike of school. Often these students will talk about how dumb school is, thus making it obvious why they wouldn't want to try; it's beneath them, not worthy of effort. It is so safe for them to hide in a cloak of not caring. If it is school that is dumb, then they are justified in adopting a superior attitude and not risking anything. The risks are huge: being made fun of, laughed at, talked about to others after class, feeling embarrassed, and, one of the worst, feeling so bad you want to cry.

However, if we fill our classrooms with signs of success, make it a room where writing a kid's name on the board means something good has happened, where kids are affirmed and encouraged, we absolutely can make it safe enough for kids to try, even fail, and try again knowing their dignity and worth are assured. Certificates on the wall listing the names of students who have achieved something are rewarding to those on the list and motivational to all the others. Regardless of the subject, teachers can create opportunities for learning that, if accomplished, can be rewarded publicly. Because I teach in a detention facility, student names are not made available to anyone outside of the school, but students derive tremendous satisfaction from the fact that other students and staff are put on notice that they have accomplished meaningful things in my class. They work hard to achieve, and they look for their names on the lists of those who have achieved; they point out their names to students and other teachers with pride.

Obviously, the poem procedure gives a great deal of recognition to students who do the work. Their names are on a Heroes/Humanitarians list on the door of the classroom. The kids' names are very, very visible, and the lists remain prominent for the entire school year and go up on the ceiling for students in future years to see. Certificates are possible for some memorization projects. A Reading for Excellence list is also prominent. I put twenty-five book titles on the list each year. When kids prove they have read and understand any of these books, they find their names on the list. In other words, success is everywhere: on the door, the walls, the ceiling. Kids succeed in room 101, and the kids know it. They can succeed, too.

> I turned a corner. Now:
> I will respect others to get respect.
> I will be loving to get love.
> I will make peace to make the world a more peaceful place.
> The street I live on, now that I've turned a corner, is named
> Hope.
> (fourteen-year-old girl)

As with the verbal affirmations mentioned in chapter 13, "Hurt People Hurt People," other positive expressions can become second nature to teacher and students alike. Success does breed success. The following words encourage success; they are public, and they create a climate of attainment:

- Well said.
- I understand.
- I hear you.
- Interesting.
- Excellent!
- You understand.
- Well done.
- Absolutely!
- Brave.
- Courageous.
- Creative.
- Thank you.

Students will pick up the practice when it becomes part of a class routine. If my classroom is known as a place where these words are used regularly, the positive message will begin to rub off on students. They will not only try harder to achieve success in the work they do in my class, they are more likely to be more generous in praising other students when they have been successful. This provides another opportunity for relationship building, which adds so much to the stability of the classroom.

15 Everyday Strategies

The 51-Percent Principle

A student must have a positive experience in class at least 51 percent of the time. This seems like a daunting challenge when dealing with kids who aren't even used to attending class 51 percent of the time. It becomes possible if the curriculum is relevant to their lives outside the classroom. In addition, solid relationships must be fostered between students and between students and teachers. If the student does not have a positive experience at least 51 percent of the time, he will not want to be in class. If he doesn't want to be there, he won't learn. Not only does he fail to contribute to anyone else's learning, his behavior is detrimental to the learning environment in the classroom.

The 51-percent principle may defy norms of teaching, but it is a guiding principle that will transform the effect of everything a teacher does. Kids who want to be in class work harder and learn more. Kids who don't will bring down the level of the learning that occurs, and the resulting mediocrity will do nothing to enhance learning. Every subject area must be relevant. Holding classroom standards high promotes success. Routinely, I make it a point to ask kids questions about their experiences in my classroom. What did you learn today? Was it interesting? What could have made it better? Are you better equipped for life by being here today? Why or why not? Honest, thoughtful feedback from students is extremely useful. When they get the message that their teacher is actually listening, they will provide surprisingly helpful input.

When the toughest kids begin to give the class high marks, the teacher knows she is making important headway by reaching kids, educating them, and making a difference. I keep the 51-percent principle firmly in mind as a primary goal for each student in each class. When I am aware of this objective, my teaching changes. It's not about me and my lesson plan, it's about the kids.

Praise in Public; Critique in Private

I was not good at ballet, and I still remember moments that made me hate ballet class. Ms. Prudence would call one of us to the front to lead the class in positions or basic techniques, all the while tapping her silver-tipped, black cane, a piano plinking in the background. When one of us, usually me, didn't do well, her tapping got louder and louder. She pointed out my failings, and I was dismissed from the front—and diminished at the front—as another student was chosen.

Ms. Prudence could have chosen other ways to correct me. By pointing out my willingness to come forward or my graceful hands, she could have salvaged much of my self-worth while still pointing out that my feet were in the wrong position before having the next student come to the front to demonstrate the correct positioning of the feet. Any good teacher will work in partnership with students to highlight strengths while correcting mistakes. A partner is encouraging and becomes a mentor, whereas a critic is just that—a criticizer—and criticism alone can be demoralizing. When students feel psychologically unsafe, they are likely to become defensive, aggressive, and threatening, or they will clam up. A student who feels safe is more likely to risk participation in class and to attempt a more cooperative attitude. That, in turn, promotes an environment where learning is more likely to occur.

When a student answers a question incorrectly, I try very hard to find something that is correct, however small the morsel may be. I may expand on it, perhaps supplementing with another fact or idea, turning it into a more accurate statement. At the very least, as facilitator, I verbally show appreciation for his contribution, modeling respect, which is the core of our classroom ethos. Even a small thumbs-up helps a young person have the courage to try again.

If a student is intentionally rude or disrespectful, I try to give a quick whisper of correction. The other kids don't hear, and the student will appreciate the privacy of the directive, especially if done with a smile. The loss when a teacher fillets a student in front of a class is permanent. Laughing at students' mistakes and sarcasm are criticisms of the worst kind. No student feels safe after that. If it can happen to one student, it can happen to anyone else. For kids to whom street cred is crucial, public critiques are deadly. Respect and trust go hand in hand; the loss of one precedes the death of the other. Everyone loses when the criticism is public.

A student must feel that it's safe and preferable to try and fail than never to try at all. I routinely show appreciation for any student's attempt at participation, striving to help him feel affirmed and of unique personal worth. By the way, students get it. Soon they, too, begin supporting other students. Nobody likes to be laughed at, and they know it. Public praise feels good and promotes class cohesion. There's enough success to go around. Mutual affirmation can become the norm.

The Archery Principle

A first-time archery student standing fifty paces from the target will likely miss when he releases the arrow. An archery student who stands with the tip of his arrow two inches from the target is bound to hit it the first time. As he takes small steps farther from the target, he will sometimes hit, sometimes miss. When he hits, he moves back. When he misses, he moves closer. He finds success.

Educators talk about individualized instruction, diagnostic placement tests, pretests, and the like. They are attempts to adapt the archery principle to the classroom. Whatever methods of diagnosing students' educational levels and needs are chosen, the underlying objective is to make educational goals attainable for each student so that there is a higher probability of success. I tell kids that the short and quick-to-administer assessments I give them are for them to see and feel proud of how much they are learning. They like to think of doing well so they can move farther from the target.

16 If We Always Teach Like We've Always Taught

America is slipping badly in education. How can we motivate kids to come to school to work hard, to learn, just like they do in other countries that are doing better than we are. All of the following are common criticisms among educators and those interested in the state of American education.

- I don't think I should have to pamper kids to make them come to school.
- Why should I have to work so hard to teach if the kids don't even care about doing well?
- I work hard every day to get these kids to learn, but I'm just not seeing results.
- In developing nations, kids work hard, often studying late into the night so they can get into good colleges. How can we compete with that?
- I'm teaching state curriculum using time-honored methods. Students better step up to the table and start learning, or they won't be able to compete internationally by the time they graduate.
- The United States doesn't rank any higher than fourteenth in any subject worldwide. It's time we get more funding for education.

There may have been a time when a teacher could have students read a chapter, answer the questions on a worksheet, and think she had done her job. I completed thousands of worksheets when I was growing up, but I don't remember learning much from them. I don't remember thinking those teachers had much impact on my life. Perhaps that style got results at a different time when the world was different. Perhaps it was considered a decent teaching style, but I don't think it is any longer.

When I was young, there were no iPads and no cell phones. There was no Internet, no YouTube, and no Facebook. Our lives were simple. Parents were involved at home, and teachers took a keen interest in our progress at school. Our parents saw to it that we were prepared for the next school day, and teachers made sure that parents were regularly apprised of how we were doing at school. This was true regardless of a family's socio-economic situation because education was seen as the way out of poverty, the key to improved status for the middle class, and the birthright for the wealthy.

Today, students live in a world of entertainment. They are bombarded with stimuli and somehow we must capture their minds, stimulate their brains, and produce young adults who can deal with the complexities of life and compete adequately with cultures from around the world. Worksheets and read-and-respond papers will only carry them so far. Is it far enough? I don't think so. I don't believe we can afford to teach like we've always taught. We need technology desperately, but we also need connection. We need information, but we need application. We need machines, but we also need human connections. We must make what they learn via

> I want your attention now
> put your name at the top of the page
> don't forget the date
> indent when you should indent
> capitalize when you should capitalize
> punctuate at the end
> read the paragraph on top
> write a one-paragraph response
> try harder
> pay attention
> be creative
> be nice
> be good
> be polite
> be quiet
> be calm
> behave
> answer the questions
> write in complete sentences
> answer every question
> guess if you don't know
> don't forget what you read
> tomorrow we will have a quiz
> don't copy off your neighbor
> don't let your neighbor copy you
> you should know how to do this
> you should have studied harder
> you should have paid attention
> If you don't do it right
>   you'll have to do it over again
> Teacher, can I live my life over again too?
>   (anonymous)

technology personal to their lives. Teachers stand in the gap. They have the treasured responsibility and opportunity to influence the future of our nation and our world.

Has the affluence in the United States taken away our drive to achieve? Has our youth culture tipped too far to right itself? Is ditching school so acceptable that excellence in schools and learning is no longer attainable? Have the demographics of the American family and culture made schooling less of a priority? Can schools be relevant to kids' lives?

The questions surrounding education in America are endless. Proposed solutions are varied and often contradictory. Will our culture evolve positively, or are we no longer going to be a world leader? Is increased funding possible and would it make any difference?

I'm not sure we can afford to wait to find out. We must do what we can do now. What we can do is make education relevant, so young people see a reason to participate. We can build relationships to ensure school is a viable place for *those* kids to attend, to belong, to learn, to achieve, and to gain the knowledge and skills they so desperately need to succeed.

17 Don't Teach a Class, Run a Program

For years I said and thought that I taught social studies or that I taught social studies classes. I still say that, but in my mind I see and feel it differently. The previous description limited me in ways I didn't even recognize. I merely thought of completing the topics listed in state curriculum standards, reading significant subject

> **An Awakening**
>
> You would think that in a place like this you would never learn anything. But here I have learned more about myself than anywhere else. My soul and my mind have been awakened. I have realized that I don't need a life of crime to be someone. All I need to be is myself, and the absolute best version of myself that I can be.
> This realization required me to awaken myself. No one else could shake me or awaken me from my sleep. It was for me to do.
> Only you can awaken you from the coma you get yourself into.
> (sixteen-year-old girl)

matter, covering topics in a timely manner, and providing assessments to measure learning. This is all good and is a respectable starting point, but it could be more.

Now I see my job as bringing the world, cultural differences, geography, history, and current events to my students. When running a program, there is a mission statement in place with goals beyond the classroom. This prepares students, using a variety of methods, to change their life paths to ensure a future that guides them away from crime and failure. This seemingly small shift keeps me constantly in the mode of retrieving knowledge, interesting ideas, and new, fresh ways of presenting learning and awareness to kids.

For learning to be relevant, topics must connect to the lives of the students, and those topics must relate to each other. This allows students to have the aha moments that are so important as education becomes more than lists on a page to memorize. If they learn about the Holocaust and the millions who were murdered because the world stood by and allowed such horror, and they learn the stories about Oskar Schindler and Irena Sender who saved thousands of people from being murdered during the Holocaust, then a discussion about the moral position of standing by while someone is forced into a gang has so much more meaning. These kids are not stupid; they are uneducated.

If one teaches the STEM curricula—science, technology, engineering, and math—imagine the new developments in these subject areas that could and should be presented daily.

The career of teaching grows with this slight paradigm shift. Teaching is big and deserves to feel that way.

18 The Worse It Gets, the Better It Becomes

I really hate to say it, but when I have a horrible, very unsuccessful day teaching kids, my frustration, disappointment, even anger, tempt me to give up, to think I can't do it. *Those* kids! They're so ungrateful. They'll never make it. They don't know anything. Their attitudes stink. Shame on those kids. They aren't learning and aren't behaving. The way they talk is disgusting. They don't care about my class. I want to double down and really make them sorry. I want to punish them, shame them, and make them pay. Of course this doesn't work and is disastrous for everyone in the room, me included. The work it takes to repair such an outburst is monumental, and a teacher may never be able to adequately undo the damage done. Even a heartfelt apology or many frank discussions do not guarantee the miracle of healing necessary for everyone to recover from the consequences of doubling down.

When I feel such frustration, anger, or despair, I must fight to regain interest and excitement about my subject and about my students. Going down to defeat goes against my grain, and looking into the faces of *those* kids reminds me of the job I am here to do. I just might come up with something new or quirky that gets everyone's attention—including mine. One of the worst days may become one of the best teaching days ever.

I was teaching the history of Russia, and one day the kids totally checked out. They were bored, and the hour plummeted into disarray and failure. I had trouble sleeping that night, but the next morning, I grabbed a matryoshka, a Russian nesting doll, and went to school. We talked about Winston Churchill, who he was and his famous quotes, including one the kids loved: "I may be drunk, Miss, but in the morning I will be sober and you will still be ugly."

Then we discussed his description of Russia in which he said, "Russia is a riddle wrapped in a mystery inside an enigma."

We stacked and unstacked the dolls relating them to Churchill's statement and to other historical events they had studied, such as the Holocaust, and to their lives. The kids were back, I was back, and excitement was back in our classroom with very little loss of time and momentum.

When everyone is out of sorts and the danger of an explosion that will do real damage is palpable, there is a great deal to be said for a break and a good night's rest. I must always remember that my goal is to reach *those* kids and that they trust me to make that happen. I can dig deep and find a way.

I hate the bad class days. I really hate them. Even more, I hate the realization that out of disaster come new visions and new enthusiasm. Okay, I love that.

19 *Those* Kids

It is difficult to put a face on *those* kids. Sometimes their posturing makes them seem dangerous and unapproachable. Their need for status with their peers, that all-important street cred, often far outweighs anything they think a teacher might do to help them. If I can relate to them and if they can learn to trust our education process, themselves, and each other, they may become dropouts of

> When people see me, they don't see me. They see a juvenile delinquent with a drug problem. You see the child begging for a second chance. You are the best teacher I've ever had. You don't see the bad in people, you only see good. That's why I think you should continue to teach here. You know how to reach kids and make them feel wanted in a place where individuality and creativity are supposed to be snuffed out like a candle.
> (fifteen-year-old girl)

another kind: not from school, but from the endless, tragic list of failing kids. When this happens, we will all be better for it.

The first day they come through the door, these kids challenge us with their words, their body language, and their attitude. Seeing them gradually, reluctantly become involved in what is happening in the classroom makes me want to wake up at 5:00 a.m. and go back every day. Where there was anger, curiosity begins to emerge. Where there was boredom, excitement. Where there was despair, hope. Initially, bullying; now, support for others. Once, certainty of failure; now, willingness to risk.

They see the possibility of no longer being defined by past mistakes. They realize they have the opportunity to make choices that will decide their future. These kids are inspired by the constant reminders in my class of the promise of a future that could be better than their past if they are willing to work for it.

I have no illusions about our ability to reach all of these kids, but far too many are deemed losers, and the system gives up on them. It is clear from the stories of these children—yes, they are still children—that many of them have been set up for failure. Detention facilities are filled with sad stories that were unbelievable to me when I started working in one. I had no idea that parents and trusted adults forced very young children to have sex with them or sold their own kids for drug money. I didn't know that sometimes the only bonding a son had with his dad was when they did drugs or committed crimes together.

I would not have imagined a family that kept a bowl of cocaine, from which the kids took a hit each day before going to school, on a coffee table in their living room. The stories of many kids have broken my heart, and I want to reach them before their lives are ruined or ended. Unless we resolve to take a new approach with these young people, they, in growing numbers, will continue to disrupt whole classrooms of kids, all of whom need a good education if they are to lead this country into the future. Behind their "looking hard" (looking tough) masks, hurting kids are determined to make others feel as miserable as they do.

The media stories most of us see do not tell about the teachers, prosecutors, judges, social workers, and other professionals who are rooting for these kids to make it and working hard to support them. *Those* kids were not born bad, but by the time they are teens, before they get to courts and correction programs, they are primed for failure and have either given up or are filled with rage. In most cases, nearly everyone—parents, teachers, friends—has marked them as lost causes or they are afraid of them.

As the process of reaching kids in order to teach them takes hold, *those* kids become *our* kids. The energy in the classroom can be contagious. Every step they—*those* kids—take toward a future where they are making safer, smarter choices, and respecting themselves and others represents hope.

Perhaps their own words will give a richer sense of these young people who struggle, sometimes haltingly, often eloquently, to speak the truth of their lives. These samples of their writings are not the most extreme or dramatic. They simply represent the kids I try to reach and to whom I try to present education that is relevant.

Choices

Choices are determiners of life
much like a decision.
Choices are what can make you do good
instead of ending up in prison.
Life is choices
Life's not chance.
Choices can turn you away from bad.
Choices can suck away so much that's sad.
Choices can be to do the right thing.
My life's necklace will have a joyful song to sing.

Amy

Miss, I am starting the second book I have ever read in my life. Thank you.

Edwardo

A Senseless Fatality

There's a problem with my thoughts today
And what that is, it's hard to say
Depression, anxiety, despair, or madness
In a one word sum, this all is sadness.

Am I losing my grip on reality?
Is my mind becoming a fatality?
I can't quite tell you how I feel,
but I do know this is one hell of an ordeal.

I'm so caught up with all my guilt,
That my perception of this world just tilts & tilts.
I keep on thinking "if I could just go back,"
But to be honest, what would I take back.

The choices I've made may have me damned,
But all in all, I am who I am.
For both the good & bad, I'll have you know,
I only show what I want to show.

Don't try to play me, don't try to save me
Because in my life, I've come to see,
That you will be you, & I will be me.

Though my mind may slip into dismay,
I've wrapped my mind around this thought today;
You cannot change what has been done,
So focus on each day, one by one.

Robert

I never knew that some people in the world have it
so much tougher than we do in America.
Now I want to be someone to help people who live like that.

Angel

R.I.P. the Old Me

In a sober mind state only clear
Thru my eyes, I was trapped in
A world of pain only liquor
Could satisfy.
With every shot I took I felt
More alive, while the angel on
My shoulder slowly died.
Now she's gone I'm alone with
The echoes of her cries,
The devil takes her place telling
Me her warnings were all lies.
Without her in the way of putting
My habits to an end,
Under the devils control liquor
Became my best friend.
Satisfied with his work the
Devil just waits, he knows
There's no room for me behind

Heaven's gates.
I chose to seek the devil and gave
Him the spot near my ear,
My reality seems fiction
And what is real becomes unclear.
Now what was wrong is right
What was cold is colder,
Because I killed that
Angel on my shoulder.

Victor

Family is everything. It can make or break you. Family broke me into pieces. Made me feel like I was nothing, had nothing, like I couldn't be nothing. I turn my back on my family like my family turned their back on me. If success is attitude and by how we respond to problems I know I have to fix myself first and then I hope I can help us be a family again.

Selena

I can't sleep cuz at night I remember. I never had someone you'd call dad. He took off when I was 6 months old and I didn't see him for 11 years.

Why did I let him do the things he did? I feel like I need protection. I started self-harming when I was 8. I pee the bed every night and he'd threaten my ass, showed me the belt and everything. I can't sleep, at all.

Gabe

Questions I'll Remember

A class of criminals who weren't seen as criminals.
    We have potential?
Before I was blind.
    I knew failure was fatal.
Can I obtain knowledge?
    Will I feel power?

I was blind to opportunities that really did exist
    I thought I had it worse.
I now make some choices

>   I have some control
> I can rise up
>   and I will succeed.

Daeshawn

A Place Called Hell

I'm in this place called hell with no one to love but everyone to hate. This world doesn't seem so great but this is the life, the life that I lead. This is a story, a story of greed for a boy with no soul who felt empty and cold cause nobody cared for the boy with no soul for he had no love in his life just sorrow and pain. He felt like he had nothing to gain with no one to pick him up when he was down he sank deeper and deeper below the ground for his life was of gaining money and fame and a life in the gang but look where it got the boy with no soul in this hell. For at first there was love then there was pain and nothing to gain but money and fame so his life is of no worth to himself but just an old toy sitting on the shelf for no father to love or protect when in need. He gained a sense of hatred indeed and his life is of pain and greed. Is there anyone to care for the boy with no soul who always feels empty and cold? So now you know of the boy with no soul who always was empty and cold.

JLS

An Analogy between a River and a Pond

A river is a moving body of which is constantly changing its surroundings and finding its way to its destination. It will carve out the earth and flow through any path it finds and it always finds the quickest route. The river is constantly striving to reach a place where it wants to be, whereas a pond is still and makes no attempt to change or be better. It is limited to its surroundings and the only change it will experience is a change that some external force will place upon it.

As my life is right now, I am a pond with limited ability to change. But if I go through with my plans for life, then I will become the river, always striving to reach my final destination. If I remain a pond, then I will go through the same cycle for the rest of my life: jail, drugs, alcohol, institutions, death. But if I strive to turn my pond to a river, then I will be able to get to where I want to be.

Richard

Forgiving people is the hardest thing in the world. If you don't forgive them they will always have power over you. How you know you've forgiven people is if you don't wake up angry at night and don't feel sick when you think about them. It really is the hardest thing to do.

Justine

Just Press Play

It's a sobering experience, being here. My life's momentum is slowed to a stop.

My life is on pause. It gives me a chance to look at my life, my choices. What is more dazzling than the choices that lay in my future, is the choices that have forged the locks on the doors. The intriguing thing is the underlying reason behind my choices. My battle with alcoholism had caused me to make the wrong choice time and time again. It's like a shower just waiting to be turned on and shower me with success and happiness, but as long as I drink I stay dry with no direction and loneliness. Now as I stand at the crossroads of my life, I have all the wisdom not to have to cry for the boy who is lost and all alone but to inherit all the riches of the world I have missed out on all this time.

Fabian

Piece by Piece

Tattered & torn
Alive & well,
I feel unborn,
So many times I fell.

Living to die,
And dying to live,
How much more do I have to give.

Forget these thoughts,
And all I have been taught.
I seem to be caught
Because of all I sought.

Let this go,
don't let it show.
I wanna save face,
I feel I'm going so slow.

Tattered & torn
Alive & well,
I feel unborn,
So many times I fell.

Living to die,
And dying to live,
How much more do I have to give.

Amanda

Epilogue

This morning a boy named Joshua told me he has always carried a gun. "Always?" I asked.

"Well, Miss, this is how it went. When I was ten, my little sister—she was seven—ran into my momma's bedroom one morning because we were out of cereal; we were out of everything, and I sent her in to ask what we could have for breakfast. But when my sister ran into momma's room, a man I had never seen before sat up in momma's bed and shot her. I don't remember much else about that morning, but I do remember that after I got my siblings to school, I bought myself a gun. I've been strapped (armed) ever since. I knew it was up to me to take care of the little kids.

> It's a joke man
> You thought you got me
> I was 8 running into my mother's room
> Shot by a man I'd never even seen
> It's a joke mom
> When you said you loved us
> but you cooked meth by the mac 'n cheese
> It's a joke sis
> you a little girl who couldn't put on your own shoes
> It's a joke on me
> Thinking I could take care and be the man.
> It's a joke school
> It's a joke and I ain't laughing
> (fifteen-year-old boy)

"You see, I was a crack baby. I have no idea who my dad was and my momma is still a crackhead. That's just the way it is. When I was twelve, one day when I brought my brothers and sisters home from school, I saw another strange man in our kitchen with Momma. They had a huge pot on the stove next to yesterday's leftover mac and cheese. He was teaching my momma to make meth, so I shot him." "Oh, Joshua," I said, "Did you kill him?" His flat response was, "I don't think so, but he never came back." Josh's life continued downhill.

We sat and talked as he tried to make some sense of his life as he worried about his younger siblings, who now didn't have their big brother at home to care for them. We talked about what it's like to grow up without a dad. He had never thought much about it. None of his friends had a dad in the home. No one in his gang—he had joined, or was jumped in, back when he was still eight—had a dad at home either.

The more we talked, the more interested he became in understanding what his unique home life meant for his past and his future. We researched the statistics, and he began to comprehend that he was one of an epidemic of fatherless teenagers growing up in America today.

We watched President Obama's speech "My Brother's Keeper." Joshua asked if some other students could join us in this study, and we ended up with a group of eight young men. Together, we embarked on a desperate search for meaning and for survival. We also broached growing up without a mother or with one who didn't adequately protect her children either because of her own choices or addiction to drugs or alcohol. Three of the eight students had a nonfunctioning mother. Five of the eight, however, had a grandmother who was their lifeline to a possible future.

This study group met for a total of about twelve hours. It was time out of my already very full day. Was it worth it? The answer is an unequivocal yes. I invested twelve hours working with these boys. They, in turn, invested themselves in my classes. Before the study group, these young men presented considerable discipline problems; afterwards, they not only didn't present discipline problems, they set a high standard for other students to aspire to. Before, they were *those* kids. After, they were kids any of us would be pleased to have in class.

Writing this book has been a labor of love, of respect for those engaged in education, and of passionate hope for reaching and teaching kids who are at risk of falling through the gaping cracks of our society.

Getting to know kids and creating lessons that contain a kernel of their lives, while remaining true to core educational principles, are critical to the journey from *those* kids to *our* kids. We all triumph.

How do we teach *those* kids?

First, we reach them.

Acknowledgements

"Write a book, Miss," a student told me. "I'm seventeen, and I'm finally learning something. I wouldn't ditch school if I had you on the outs." Although many students give teachers wonderful comments about their teaching skills, Richie became really persistent during his long stay at a school where I taught. It became a chorus from his classmates that was heartening to me, and it planted a seed. The lessons I learned teaching lost kids have applications for virtually any school, anywhere.

I want to thank my students who, during the past fourteen years, brought increased meaning to my life and, without a doubt, taught this teacher how to teach. My hope is that what I have learned, and have seen succeed, can and will enrich the national focus on improving education, our schools, and the lives of young people.

My editor, Marilyn Huff Mullen, is a lifelong friend. We met the first day of kindergarten, and I have always felt gratitude for her friendship and wisdom. During this project, she has become an invaluable, professional resource with incredible expertise in editing and styling a manuscript. Her intellect and skill in project management give her an extra degree of astuteness when envisioning the potential in the manuscripts she takes under her wing. Her sensitivity in guiding me through the final phases has been a godsend. Her persistence is legendary; her guidance, truthful. I am grateful that my lifelong friend is now my editor.

Partway through life, I met a person who was to become a sister, advisor, and confidante. Barbara Cole is the most positive and affirming person I have ever known. Her work in education and teen counseling has redeemed, even salvaged, the lives of those fortunate to have encountered this extraordinary human being. The trail she leaves behind her is strewn with gratitude and mended lives—mine included.

Another positive force in my life has been Jim Birschbach, known to all as coach, mentor, and friend. He has been all of these to me and to my family.

Dr. Dan Hansen, an early encourager of this book, always thinks I can do anything. He hears my stories and, as a mentor himself to troubled youth, understands the passion I have for this work. His confidence in me bolsters my courage when the challenge seems particularly difficult.

Michelle Jordan and my fellow teachers at the detention center school challenge and inspire me each day to bring my A game, to teach in a manner that can change and encourage those kids to live lives with responsibility and meaning. They are an extraordinary group of dedicated, highly skilled professionals.

Dr. Tom Davidson, a trusted consultant, never gave me the solutions, but taught me to search for them, illusive as they often were. This journey generated growth that has been authentic and life-giving.

On a wonderful day in central Texas, I met a charming and caring man, General James L. Dozier. He became a trusted adviser to me and to my sons. In good times and bad I can turn to this always decent and wise man. I am grateful.

Ms. Janet Culloton's skills in editing, together with her deep understanding of the education and learning processes, have been invaluable in the publishing of this book. She is a calm, yet masterful copy editor, which is soothing to an author who understands the need for her precision, but will never desire or aspire to the talent she possesses.

Several years ago I began monthly Saturday breakfast meetings with a group of writers I now call my band of brothers. We are all passionate about writing and have become friends who support each other as we each work to fulfill the dream of completing our various projects. Without their genuine concern and generous advice, I would not have had the guts to face my own fears and finish this book. To them I am deeply grateful.

And finally, I salute the champions of excellence who have brought the quality of education to the forefront of American discourse. These outspoken leaders and resources have prompted me to teach differently, better, and in styles their words have encouraged. They include:

- Michelle Rhee, founder of StudentsFirst and author of *Radical: Fighting to Put Students First*
- Geoffrey Canada, president of Harlem Children's Zone and author of *Reaching Up for Manhood: Transforming the Lives of Boys in America* and *Fist Stick Knife Gun: A Personal History of Violence*
- The film *Raising Cain: Exploring the Inner Lives of America's Boys*, a PBS documentary, based on the book *Raising Cain: Protecting the Emotional Life of Boys* written by Dan Kindlon, PhD, and Michael Thompson, PhD
- Documentary film *Bully* directed by Lee Hirsch
- Documentary film *Waiting for "Superman"* directed by Davis Guggenheim

These giants of education and cultural reform have brought creative thinking to media, to board rooms, and to the kitchen table. The benefits to our children are immeasurable.

About the Author

Mary Duerksen Sklar was raised in a family that valued education. For years, as a young girl, she thought that *doctor* was a first name since it applied to so many of the guests in her childhood home. Family members included a grandfather who studied medicine in Vienna, a grandmother who was among the first woman graduates of the Chicago Art Institute, and her brother who was paid to attend the University of Michigan for graduate work in chemistry. Her father was dean of the School of Fine Arts at Wichita State University; educators, musicians, and cultural leaders were frequent dinner guests, and conversation was rich and stimulating.

In her adult life, Mary was a mother to her two sons, Trey and Andy, and raised them while moving around the country and the world to places as diverse as Washington, D.C.; Monterey, California; Mainz, Germany; and Moscow, Russia. In Moscow, Mary taught English in a large, neighborhood school. Intending just to help the Russians, she herself was deeply impressed with the perspective they had of education as a privilege, not only a right, and the strong family ties to the school and community.

More recently, Mary spent more than a decade teaching social studies in a youth detention center in Colorado. These were kids who were hard to love, but so in need of the special gifts Mary brought to the classroom. They are tough, but few could resist her relentless enthusiasm for life, her love for learning, and her determination to help each student take pride in his work and talents. The pages of this book are inspired by her experiences learning to teach, influence, and, in many ways, love *those* kids.

www.ingramcontent.com/pod-product-compliance
Lightning Source LLC
LaVergne TN
LVHW021348080426
835508LV00020B/2164